D1006695

Client Testimonials for Allen Roland's Transformation Counseling

"Working with Allen started an avalanche of personal growth for me. It got me moving, clearing up many roadblocks that had been holding me back, in some cases for decades. I had more insight and movement from that series of sessions than I had in the previous ten years. The feelings of liberation, self-confidence and sheer joy of living are almost indescribable!"

—David Simonson *Reno, Nevada*

"The work I did with Allen Roland has been truly transformational. The seven sessions forced me to deal with core personal issues—issues that affected my ability to fully be present and enjoy myself to my fullest ability. Having completed these sessions I am now fully embracing my family and relationships around me."

—Leland Whitney *San Francisco, California*

"If you have not had the opportunity to work with Allen, read this book! If you have read it—read it again! My experience of Allen's work was profound. It has allowed me, and everyone I know who is willing to take on the challenge of truly loving, to connect with others in a way that would have been impossible prior to this work. Allen deserves sainthood for all the people he has personally empowered."

— Judy Foley, President, The Patricia Moore Group, Inc.
San Francisco, California

"One has to be ready to embrace their own fears in order to experience the truth. My sessions with Allen have brought me full circle. Facing and going through my own fears has significantly enabled me to become a fuller, more complete person. I now feel that I deserve to be happy, and my life has become a celebration!"

—Donna Shadowens *Novato, California*

TO TINA
With love + joy

[signature]
3/02/02

radical
therapy

radical therapy

by

Allen L. Roland, PhD

Surrender to love
and heal yourself
in seven sessions
(not seven years)

Origin Press

Novato, California

Origin Press

1122 Grant Avenue, Suite C • Novato, CA 94945
1.888.267.4446 • OriginPress.com

Publisher's Cataloging-in-Publication
(Provided by Quality Books, Inc.)

Roland, Allen L.
    Radical Therapy : surrender to love and heal yourself
in seven sessions (not seven years) /Allen L. Roland
—1st ed.
    p. cm.
    Includes bibliographical references.
    LCCN: 2001088563
    ISBN: 1-57983-006-4

    1. Self-actualization (Psychology). 2. Change
(Psychology) 3. Love. I. Title.

BF637.S4R65 2001   158.1
                    QBI01-700904

Printed in the United States of America
10 9 8 7 6 5 4 3 2 1

Dedication

This book is dedicated to children everywhere, who deeply sense their joyful connection to a state of soul consciousness (the Unified Field) and must decide for themselves if it is their imagination or reality.

This book is also dedicated to Albert Einstein, Carl Jung, Pierre Teilhard de Chardin, and Joseph Allen Bryant. They were, in a sense, my mentors from beyond time and space. Each of them inspired me to find and share this truth: that the basic uniting and underlying force of the universe is a psychic energy field of love and soul consciousness (the Unified Field) which lies not only beyond time and space but also beneath our deepest fears.

Albert Einstein looked at nature in awe and wonder and dared to think the unthinkable. He always believed that a common pattern was there to be seen if one could look with the fresh, clear eyes of a child.

Carl Jung sensed a parallel between theoretical physics and depth psychology. This inspired his efforts to probe the deepest regions of his own psyche, as well as that of others, in search of a unifying source of energy and a causal theory of sychronicity comparable in scope to Einstein's theory of relativity.

Pierre Teilhard de Chardin clearly defined this all-unifying source of energy as *love*.

Joseph Allen Bryant, my beloved grandfather, gave me the conscious, unconditional love that opened my heart as a young child. His loving presence and spirit served as a source of inspiration and a beacon of light on my journey of surrender through the darkness to the love, joy, and intention deepest within myself.

I am again the little boy who could feel love for his grandfather literally leaping from his heart. That love, I now know, joined him, and now joins me, to a Unified Field of love that extends to all humankind.

This book is an expression of that love.

Contents

Acknowledgments

I have many people to thank for helping to make this book a reality, yet little space in which to do so.

My thanks must start with Stanley Krippner. He sensed my destiny in 1972 and directed me to numerous people who have helped me on my journey. One is Grace Petitclerc, who taught me that standing alone and singing my song was really belonging. Another is Byron Belitsos, my publisher. I am indebted to Byron for having the courage to publish, and to bring his vision, purpose, and remarkable editing skills to this book.

The foundation of this book is my 1998 dissertation entitled "The Unified Field." The dissertation could not have been accomplished without the guidance, insight, and support of my mentor and friend Mary Schmitt, PhD.

Heartfelt thanks to Doug Childers, my editor, who brought skills, joy, and good humor to the demanding process of shifting the emphasis of this book from an award-winning dissertation to an inspirational book on self-healing.

A special acknowledgment goes to Phillip Dizick, whose artistic creative genius brought magic to the cover design and layout of this book.

Another acknowledgment goes to Laurie Pietsch, whose unselfish dedication and editing skills brought life, immediacy, and authenticity to my session chapters.

Thanks also to both Esther Riley and Antera, whose suggestions and copyediting were instrumental in completing this book.

A special acknowledgment to all my clients who have allowed me to touch them deeply and, in turn, have touched me deeply and inspired me to fully own my truth. A very special acknowledgment goes to my soul sister, Diana Dubrow, for her continued encouragement and support.

Last, but certainly not least, a most special acknowledgment to the great loves of my life. In allowing me to fully surrender to love and let go with love when it became appropriate, they helped set the stage for me to fully embrace myself, share my truth, and open my heart to the universe.

God reveals Himself only to a grateful heart. A God of love has been revealed to me, and my heart is filled with awe, wonder, and humbleness at not only knowing such a great truth—but also for having the opportunity to share it with you.

My last acknowledgment is to you, dear reader. By reading this book, you will set the stage to heal yourself by surrendering to love.

—Allen L. Roland, PhD

Foreword

The dictionary contains many definitions for the word "radical," one of which is "proceeding from the root, reaching for the center or ultimate source." This is exactly the approach taken by Allen Roland's book, *Radical Therapy,* an inspirational and radical tool for self-healing. It is, in fact, a brilliant work from the heart, one that will touch and challenge you to the core.

The very root of Allen's therapy involves opening one's heart through a profound surrender to love. Allen's model of the "Unified Field of love" was originally developed in a dissertation (for which I was an advisor) that was named one of the best of the year by a panel of judges appointed by the Institute of Noetic Sciences and the magazine *Common Boundary.* I had worked with Allen earlier, in 1972, and am gratified by the reports given me by some of the clients who have benefited from his innovative counseling practice.

Radical Therapy offers its readers seven cathartic sessions. These self-directed activities offer powerful tools that rest upon a key proposition: Affirming our most authentic feelings, intuitions, and convictions, regardless of the consequences, facilitates healing. This risk taking inspires people to encounter their deepest fears, confront their grief, and to discover the love and integration that these emotions have been blocking.

These seven sessions can be undertaken alone, with a friend, with a spiritual advisor, as a member of a group, or as a client of a counselor or psycho-therapist.

The sessions are geared to enable the reader to plug into the Unified Field of love, and derive its benefits. Many other writers have spoken of similar connections that link all humanity—indeed, all sentient beings. For example, Alan Watts insisted that people are more than "skin-encapsulated egos"; Rupert Sheldrake has proposed "morphic fields" that cannot be seen, but which are known through their effects. I have encountered this model many times during my work in parapsychology, shamanism, and altered states of consciousness. In our book *The Mythic Path*, David Feinstein and I write about "mythic fields," and cite a dozen research projects whose data support the notion that there are areas of influence that bypass conventional ideas about personal boundaries. Allen's unique contribution is the application of this model to spiritual counseling, helping people to escape dysfunctional relationships and to avoid habitual behavior patterns that have inhibited their innate joy and happiness.

Over the years, I have spoken with many indigenous shamans who work with members of their community who have "lost their souls." Sometimes these souls have been lost through trauma, sometimes through betrayal, sometimes through sorcery, and sometimes through self-destructive activities. The shaman will take a "shamanic journey" to search for these missing souls and, upon retrieving them, will conduct a ritual in which the souls are returned and their owners are made whole.

No psychiatric manual lists "soul loss" as a condition in need of treatment, but shamans tell me that "soul loss" is widespread in contemporary society. Allen Roland has had the insight to understand what the shamans have told me. He also has developed the skills to help his clients regain their souls. What he has learned and practiced during the past quarter of a century is available to those who read this book. I would urge its readers to take advantage of this opportunity and to embark on a journey of self-discovery and self-integration.

—Stanley Krippner, PhD
Saybrook Graduate School

*The basic underlying
and uniting force of the universe
is a psychic energy field of love and
soul consciousness (the Unified Field)
which lies not only beyond time
and space but also beneath
our deepest fears.*

—Allen Roland

radical therapy

1

how you can use this book to heal yourself

If your everyday practice is to open to all your emotions, to all the people you meet, to all the situations you encounter, without closing down, trusting that you can do that—then that will take you as far as you can go.

And then you'll understand all the teachings that anyone has ever taught.

—Pema Chodron

Radical Therapy shows you how to heal yourself by *opening* your heart through a profound surrender to love, through a simple act of saying yes to your deepest feelings—*yes to who you really are.*

Saying yes means having the courage to express your truest feelings, and requires that you live from your deepest convictions. Saying yes to who you really are puts an end to a life controlled by fear.

My work as a radical therapist has proven to me that when we surrender to love by courageously going through our deepest fears and pain, our hearts will open and we will discover our authentic self—that is, the love, joy, and intention that is our original birthright. We will gain access to a profound state of consciousness—I call it *soul consciousness*—that we once knew as children. We will in fact enter into what I call the *Unified Field of love*—a universal ocean of love that exists beyond time and space and which surrounds and infuses all things.

The seven sessions described in this book—if you go through them with courage and determination—have the potential to *jump-start your heart.* They will allow you to surrender to love and reunite with the Field. You may use this book as a tool in your work with a therapist, a spiritual counselor, a healing group, or a friend; but it is also designed to be used without outside assistance for those courageous readers who are determined to heal themselves.

The Unified Field of love and soul consciousness exists within each of us—*beneath our deepest fears and grief—and also beyond death, time, and space.* The Field reveals itself in near-death experiences, in mystic states, to all children everywhere, and to those who say yes to their deepest feelings and surrender to love. The poet Longfellow described it as "the thread of all-sustaining beauty that runs through all and doth all unite."

In other words, each of us is a living portal whose hidden depths open onto the Unified Field of love that is our common source.

Radical Therapy organically emerged out of my own healing journey. By finally surrendering to love and going through my deepest fears, I experienced the Unified Field of love and soul consciousness that was hidden beneath those fears. I reconnected to that state of inner unity we all experienced in our earliest child-hood, and most likely even in the womb. And this very process became the foundation of my work with others as a therapist.

Even now, after 25 years as a therapist working with clients from all walks of life, I am amazed to see, over and over again, how simple it is for us to heal our-selves emotionally by fully surrendering to the love and joy that is deepest within us. My work has proven to me that we can each return to the soul consciousness that lives within us as our *original* self. We can become again the joyous and open-hearted children we once were. It really is that simple!

But the path to soul consciousness is the path of the heart, and living from the heart requires great courage. For you to truly heal yourself you must confront and go through your darkest fears—and you must stop being a victim by taking full accountability for your life. You must realize that you alone are responsible for the decisions you made to close your heart and settle for less than all of yourself. Only then can you joyfully claim your place in the universal loving plan in which you may now be a reluctant participant.

Until we fully heal, our adult relationships tend to reflect the deprivations we experienced as children with our parents or primary caregivers. Our romantic love relationships in particular become like grade D movies as we re-enact the same miserable dramas and childhood traumas over and over again.

The lessons of our relationships are a key focus of my work for several reasons: Intimate relationships are the litmus test—the literal testing ground—of our ability to surrender, open our heart, and move beyond our fears. *Only in relationship can we free ourselves from fear.* It was in relationship with our primary caregivers that we first became seemingly separated from love and where we first began to give in to fear and say no to our truest selves. So we began at a very early age to look outside—in relationships with parents, siblings, and others —for the inner validation we once had but lost and which is now hidden beneath an inner black hole of fear and pain that we are too afraid to confront or even feel.

I chiefly concentrate on feelings in my work, for only the full surrender to and expression of *the primal feelings of our woundedness* can lead us through our deep-est fears to the ultimate feeling—love. Feelings are the thread we must follow to the love and joy at our core. And love is the ultimate feeling, the living pulse of our innate connection to the Unified Field of love, which is our common source.

I am convinced that all children experience this state of love and soul consciousness. I believe that it is even present in our prenatal condition, for at birth we all emerge from this Unified Field of love.

But in a short time we all become absorbed and finally trapped in the limits of conventional ego con-sciousness. Gradually, what our parents and teachers tell us becomes "reality"—and the truth we once felt and intuitively knew becomes a figment of our imagina-tions. Unable to really see us for who we uniquely are, those on whom we depend for love and survival proj-ect their own wounded selves onto us. And we as young children inevitably receive these projections, and are wounded in turn; we then become whatever we think we have to become in order to be loved and to survive. And so our life becomes a quest to overcome this conditioning and return to our original state of soul consciousness.

I spend most of the first session in my private practice explaining the paradigm in which my work is done. The first stage is *preparation,* the necessary first step toward healing. The second step is *action*, or engag-ing the healing/transformational processes described in this book. The third and final stage is *integration*, where listening to and following your own inner guidance leads to inner validation. This stage replaces the need for external guidance and outer validation that caused us, as children, to abandon our true selves.

The primary purpose of this book, therefore, is to demonstrate that beneath our deepest fears is a state of love, joy, and soul consciousness; that this love is the ultimate totalization of human energy, or the Unified Field of love itself; and that when we surrender through our deepest fears to this universal well of joy that lives within each of us, we are healed and transformed. We can all experience the same state of consciousness that Jesus, Buddha, and other great masters manifested in their lives if we will fully and finally surrender to love.

Using the seven powerful sessions presented in this book (which include exercises and homework), I have helped hundreds of people to emerge from cocoons of fear into greater aliveness, to move from a place of painfully separated ego consciousness to the place of inner unity and belonging that I call soul consciousness. These sessions are designed to help you heal yourself and fully open your heart by leading you through your own deepest fears and pain to the well of joy at your core. For only this depth of healing can end the unconscious re-enactments of unresolved childhood traumas, within which most of us spend the remaining years of our lives.

All my clients are referrals, and my average client

is finished in seven two-hour sessions over five to six days or a few weeks, depending on the client's availability. As a result of my own experience and my work with others, having seen that most people—with the right support and guidance—are capable of healing themselves in this way, I have become firmly convinced that *most long-term therapy is nothing more than thinly disguised codependency.*

We therapists cannot take anyone any further than we have gone ourselves. To help our clients learn to trust themselves, we must be able to move beyond our own fears and our need to control. I am convinced that to really help our clients heal themselves, we must be able to deeply connect to them from a place of soul consciousness. Only then can we effectively make contact with the emotionally trapped and lonely child in others.

By just such a deep and honest interchange of thoughts and feelings—or soul-to-soul communion— I inspire my clients to find the inner courage to own and fully express their long-suppressed, "forbidden" feelings and to pass consciously through their deepest fears to a place of inner joy, intention, and love that exists on the "other side" in all of us.

My only job as their "coach" (a term I prefer to "therapist"), is to empower them on this courageous path through their fears until they begin to feel the growing joy of inner validation. I call it *Transformation Counseling.* Because this is client-centered therapy and because the inner transformation usually begins to take place in only two or three sessions, I like to say that I jump-start the hearts of my clients. This work enables them to discover and heal the child within themselves, to open their hearts to the people closest to them, and, more and more, to open their hearts to others.

If you use this book as your guide and allow me to be your coach, and really engage the seven sessions outlined here—the very same ones I lead my clients through—you will go through a process of inner transformation. By that I mean that you will begin to fully open your heart, heal yourself, and discover the joy that is deepest within you. But you must do the work. The best I can do is help you get to a place of choice, a place of deep soul-based inner validation versus ego-based outer validation. The work presented step-by-step in these pages will allow you to experience this option. But it is up to you to choose.

Besides this primary therapeutic/transformational purpose, *Radical Therapy* has a secondary purpose: to show that my theory of a Unified Field of love answers the search for a grand Unified Field theory of modern physics. My research, personal experience, and psychological work with clients have shown me that there is a deep underlying and unifying force in the universe, an infinite energy field of love and soul consciousness in which all other forces of nature are merely conditions of state. And this infinite field of love—and not the speed of light—*is the absolute constant of the universe.* My theory of a Unified Field of love joyfully proclaims that psychology, science, and religion all rest on a common foundation of *love*.

The Unified Field theory that I propose has much corroborative evidence, some of which I will present in the coming chapters. However, in this book I intend to establish its plausibility and demonstrate its implications and applications only for the purposes of psychological healing and spiritual transformation.

There is every reason for human beings to undertake this healing journey through the underworld of their fears and pain. But the best reason is that *love is the deepest part of who we are.*

I heartily invite you to take this great journey of healing with me. Read each chapter carefully, dynamically engage each of the seven sessions, and do the homework and exercises as if your life depends on it.

Because, in a way, it does.

2

the
search
for the
Unified
Field

The great philosophical triumph of any unified field theory is implicit in the first word of its title. For it will carry to logical fulfillment the long course of science towards the unification of man's concepts of the physical world. For from its august perspective the entire universe would appear as one elemental field in which each atom, each flying electron, each star, each wandering comet and slow-wheeling galaxy, is seen to be but a ripple or tumescence in the underlying space-time unity.

And so a profound simplicity would supplant the surface complexity of nature. Thus all man's

*perceptions of the world and all his abstract intu-
itions of reality would merge finally into one, and
the deep underlying unity of the universe would be
laid bare.*
—Lincoln Barnett

I have proposed in the first chapter that the fundamental underlying and uniting force of the universe
is an *infinite* psychic energy field of love and soul consciousness and that it lies not only beyond time and
space but also within each of us, beneath our deepest
fears. Yet, can it really be a scientific fact that love
underlies and unites all things? Isn't this just some new
form of mysticism? Can it really be this simple?

The hypothesis of the Unified Field of love vali-
dates the reports of mystics who directly (and *subjectively*) experienced the same reality that scientists only
approach through an *objective* and outward process of
observation, experimentation, and deduction. In other
words, the same phenomena that science describes as
"energy" or "light" can be directly experienced as love
—*if experienced from within*. In other words, light is a
constant of the physical universe, as Einstein showed,
but love is the absolute constant of the universe, as the
heart reveals.

Coming to such a conclusion is, of course, relative
to your state of consciousness and is entirely observer-
dependent. In radical therapy, I help my clients open
their hearts and *experience directly* (meaning *subjectively*)
their deepest inner connection to this universe of love.

And it is my hope that scientists will realize just how this truth is observer-dependent, and will be able as a result to link this subjective experience of the Unified Field with their own more limited theories, based on their objective observation of nature.

But can it really be this simple—that love is the absolute constant of the universe? I not only believe this; I know that it is! And I believe that Albert Einstein, who first set in motion the search for the Unified Field theory, and who mistrusted complicated theories, would have been delighted with this truth. For he believed that the simplest explanation of any physical phenomenon was sure to be the right one. Accordingly, the solution to the search for a Unified Field theory that he spent his last years futilely seeking would seemingly have to be a simple one.

Stephen Hawking, like his predecessor Einstein, has also sought a simple explanation for the Unified Field. "What is it that breathes fire into the equations and makes a universe for them to govern?" Hawking writes. "Is the ultimate Unified Field so compelling that it brings about its own existence?"[1]

Those who live from the heart know the answer: That which breathes fire into all of the equations is a *universal energy field of love.* Yes, love is so compelling that it does indeed bring about its own existence, and the existence of all things.

Hawking also wrote that there ought to be something special and simple about a grand theory of everything. *And what could be more special and simple than love?*

For me, as a therapist and a man who lives from the heart, the deep underlying unity of the universe has been laid bare: There is indeed a Unified Field of love underlying and sustaining this vast universe. This love is the creative force within cosmic and biological evolution, within each human being, and within the very cells and atoms of which all matter is composed. I believe this is the simplest and most profound explanation there could be.

This concept of the Unified Field of love also seems to fit within Einstein's grand aim of science, which is "to cover the greatest number of empirical facts by logical deduction from the smallest number of hypotheses or axioms."[2] Allow me therefore to introduce the central axiom that serves as the foundation for my theory of a Unified Field of love:

> Love alone is capable of uniting living beings in such a way as to complete and fulfill them, for it alone takes them and joins them to what is deepest within themselves.[3]
>
> —Teilhard de Chardin

Let us explore the rich implications of this quote from one of the last century's towering geniuses— a man who was, at one and the same time, one of our greatest scientists, evolutionary theorists, and mystics. This profound statement of Teilhard's is the essential guidepost of my work. Bearing it in mind, let us also explore the meaning of the Unified Field of love itself.

First, an undeniable and universal *urge to unite* lies deep within us all, and in fact in all things. For humans, it is the most powerful of all drives, yet it cannot be observed through the most powerful electron microscope or through the lens of the largest telescope. This urge to unite is a direct emanation from the Unified Field, a current of divine transformational energy to which we must surrender if we are to understand its qualities. This energy longs to flow through us according to its nature, and the resistance to this current of love, rising from the depths in each of us, is the source of all human suffering. To merge with this healing and transforming current we must surrender through this resistance—through our deepest fears and pain—into the Unified Field of love that is our source.

The act of expressing and receiving love fulfills and completes us by energetically uniting us to the Unified Field of love *that also unites all of creation and is at the same time deepest within ourselves.*

Yet if love is so powerful and is experienced by so many, why does it often seem not to last, and why does it leave so many lovers unhealed and untransformed? Because most people only touch, but do not fully surrender to, the love and joy that is beyond their deepest fears and pain. They love until it hurts, and when the pain comes, they close their hearts—suddenly or gradually—and withdraw, just as they did when they were children.

Why should we surrender and keep our hearts open in the face of so much fear or pain? Because it turns out that this the only way to establish and maintain our conscious connection to the Unified Field of love. *Establishing and maintaining this connection is our primary purpose in life.*

Now you might ask: What then is the ultimate purpose of the Unified Field itself? As far as I know, the purpose, the intent, is simply to love and become active participants in a loving plan. As such, *God is a loving plan in action.* Each of us, I believe, has an important part to play in this loving plan—and our ultimate joy will be knowing this and doing it!

God and the Unified Field are one and the same. In essence, the omnipresent psychic energy field of love that binds the universe is a divine state of consciousness—or what I call *soul* consciousness. As Teilhard de Chardin wrote:

> In the last analysis, somehow or other, there is something through which material and spiritual energy hold together and is complementary . . . there must be a single energy operating in the world. That something, he declared, is the soul itself.[4]

Modern physics teaches us that energy can be neither created nor destroyed but is perpetually transformed. In other words, all that exists is immortal, not in form but in essence. Likewise the soul, which is also energy in a higher and more conscious form, can be neither created nor destroyed. And it is perpetually evolving, transforming, and perfecting itself within a constantly evolving and loving plan.

The Unified Field of love is by my definition

nothing but *an ultimate or universal soul purposefully engaged in an infinite process of creation.* (And what is that but a definition of God?) We are all participating in that evolutionary process as cocreators. Love is the ultimate attractive force of the universe, holding all forms of matter together, causing all particles to dance in magnetic relation to each other. Love is the force that drives evolution. It also makes bees buzz, birds sing, lovers sigh, and heals suffering souls.

As such, both the Unified Field and the universal soul represent the attractive force of the universe, the force that holds all forms of matter and life together so that an evolving loving plan (God) can manifest itself through them. Thus soul consciousness is the awareness of an evolving loving plan and the taking of responsibility for one's function within that plan.

So why on earth would we *not* choose to surrender to this Unified Field and play our part in its loving plan? The short answer is *fear.* Soul consciousness, or our awareness of this Unified Field and its loving plan, is often buried beneath our deepest fears. Yet the urge to love and unite calls each of us out of our fear to take responsibility and play our part within that plan. Eventually, it demands that we go inside through our deepest fears and surrender to love.

All roads in our ceaseless search for external truths eventually lead back to the self, to our own sensory experience of our own state of consciousness. Love is both a state of soul consciousness and the transmutation agent by which we refine our consciousness.

Love relationships are vehicles by which our transformation from ego consciousness to soul consciousness is accomplished.

Besides our own transformation, our greater task, you might say, is to *consciously birth the Unified Field of love into this dimension.* Indeed, we are all emissaries of love on a mission to a planet that is in the process of being born into soul consciousness. Our task in this great mission is to fully open our hearts, burst out from our cocoons of ego consciousness, and finally sing our own unique song.

Our journey from ego to soul consciousness is also a journey from what I call *emotional love* to *conscious love.* The force that connects us most directly to the Unified Field is conscious love. Conscious love, which is also defined as unconditional love, desires that the loved object attain its own native perfection *regardless of the consequences to the lover.* In its highest state, conscious love, like the energy of the sun—the heart of this great atom that is our solar system—shines unconditionally on all living beings.

Emotional love, by contrast, is love that is bound by ego consciousness. It becomes threatened when the loved object moves toward its own perfection and out of the control of the lover. If it does not evolve toward conscious love, emotional love will seek to possess and control the loved object until it ultimately stifles all traces of love. The growth from emotional love to conscious love is not achieved painlessly or without conscious resolve and persistent effort. The ego, with all its fears and need to control, must be relinquished, for only then can we truly connect to the Unified Field of love, which is our source, and claim our part in the loving plan. Only then can the butterfly of our real and authentic self emerge from its cocoon.

We are all *capable by design* of consciously or unconditionally loving others. *Yet we cannot love others consciously until we consciously love ourselves.* We become capable of self-love only by allowing and sharing our deepest feelings while releasing any fears, sense of unworthiness or shame, or other barriers that separate us from the soul consciousness that is deepest within us. By doing this, we both purify and embrace our true self. Such work is the essence of self-love.

Thus our souls evolve through purification, moving from emotional love to conscious love, the soul's highest state. This transformational journey from emotional love to conscious love, or from ego consciousness to soul consciousness, is the defining purpose of our life and our significant relationships. Conscious love unites us with what is deepest within—the universal state of soul consciousness, the Unified Field. It restores our original, joyful, loving self that we once knew as children. And it allows us to finally take our place in this loving, evolving plan and fully manifest our innate connection to the Unified Field.

William James, the great 20th century philosopher/scientist, profoundly observed that the science of the future must depend upon what he called a "radical empiricism." Our journey to understand the history of the universe, he knew, must not depend only on our five senses and our scientific instruments. *To understand the nature of the universe in which we live, we must also include the evidence of our subjective inner experience. In other words, true science must include the journey of the heart toward knowing truth.* A genuine Unified Field theory must combine the objective observations of the scientist and the subjective knowing, or soul consciousness, of the mystic.

If we cannot find truth within ourselves, or trust the inner knowing that is the essence of our true self, we can never fashion a reliable science. For a science divorced from the heart will be misinterpreted by a mind that is afraid to comprehend its own essential knowing.

Join me on this inner journey of the heart to know the truth. For that is the key to your own transformation, and the essence of radical therapy!

3

my experience of the Unified Field

*It is only through the heart that one sees clearly
—what is essential is invisible to the human eye.*

—Antoine de Saint-Exupéry

As children, we all feel—or at least briefly glimpse
—the joyous state of soul consciousness. But most of us
lose touch with it, or *check out,* as I like to say, by
around the age of six. By "check out," I mean that we
emotionally stop growing and become whatever we
think we must in order to be loved. From then on, as
I have explained, we move through life as an alienated
and "false self." And so we repeatedly encounter and

recreate the place where we originally checked out in situations and relationships that trigger our original wound. Unconsciously, we grope for that authentic place we once knew as children—before we were wounded and emotionally shut down—but with limited success.

The deepest layer of this wound is our sadness over apparently not being seen, or loved, for who we were. The next layer is our anger and resentment at having to become someone we are not in order to be loved. Nevertheless, beneath this anger, sadness, and pain is the original joy we once knew—our innate state of soul consciousness and our connection to the Unified Field of love.

We all long to recover that joyful state of soul consciousness. So our life becomes a quest to return to that original place of authenticity, and to play our part in the evolving loving plan. Both we as individuals and the planet as a whole are in the process of making a shift from ego consciousness to soul consciousness.

Our task on this journey is to open our hearts emotionally, heal the child within us who originally checked out, and finally discover who we really are. But the journey doesn't really start until we *fully open our hearts*.

My whole life has been a journey, a quest, to find a lost little boy within myself who once knew, and longed to share the truths I am sharing now with you; a little boy who profoundly experienced at the deepest level within himself, a love and joy that indelibly connected him to all. That experience was my first awareness of the Unified Field of love.

The experience happened when I was four years old while playing alone in my room one glorious summer day in Newtonville, Massachusetts. At the time, I knew that I was loved and that I was special, though I was already struggling with the psychic wound of having a beautiful, spoiled, somewhat depressed mother who was emotionally unavailable to me. Already in that relationship, I intuitively knew that who I was, was seemingly not enough. (I never knew my father, who had left my mother before I was born.) I also had an identical twin brother whom I loved and who loved me. And our maid, Delia, whom I loved, also adored me. But my deepest love was for my grandfather. At times I recall feeling an incredible love leaping from within my heart toward him. My grandfather truly loved me unconditionally, and his love more than made up for the lack of love I felt from my mother.

That day in my room, I suddenly heard my favorite song on the radio—Gene Autrey's "I'm Back in the Saddle Again." My inner joy grew too great to contain. I felt an incredible urge to share it. So I turned the radio up full volume, stood on my tiptoes, opened the window, and leaned out into that gorgeous New England summer day. Immediately, an overwhelming joy seemed to lift me out of myself. An utterly amazing feeling of *knowing* rose from deep within me, a feeling of incredible joy and oneness with all things. *And I totally surrendered to it.* For a few ecstatic moments,

I sensed, knew, that I was not alone. This awesome joy lifted me out of myself and somehow connected me to all and everything.

Of course, I am not alone in having this kind of childhood experience. There is very strong evidence that preschool children have a deep and natural psychic connection with nature. In my work as a therapist, I have conducted awareness groups with children from preschool through high school. When I ask preschool children to draw a self-portrait, they will often fill the page with deer, dolphins, eagles, flowers, and the sun. They intuitively see and experience themselves as part of nature. They are relatively unafraid, uncomplicated, and unself-conscious. Most young children have little, if any, fear of expressing their love and deepest feelings for animals, for nature, for their dolls and stuffed toys, for their parents, and for each other.

Yet, by the third grade most children have all but lost this openness, this knowing connection with nature, with themselves, and with their peers. They've become more fearful and insecure about expressing their deepest feelings. The belief that being themselves is not enough has taken root in their consciousness; they have begun the inevitable surrender to what their parents and others agree is reality. Their connection to nature and to the inner well of joy that marked their infancy has begun to fade as they make the transition from soul consciousness to ego consciousness.

At four years old, I knew—for one instant—that I was a beloved and essential part of a loving universe.

Two years later, when I was suddenly taken away from my grandfather, my heart closed and I checked out. Emotionally, I stopped growing. For the next 30 years the transcendent moment of soul consciousness I had experienced remained buried beneath a well of grief, a mantle of psychic pain, aloneness, and despair. After the trauma of losing my beloved grandfather, it hurt too much to feel anything deeply. Closing my heart was the beginning of my surrender to the adult version of reality and my entry into ego consciousness. In the face of more psychic pain than I could handle—a place of no choice—this was my only option for survival.

No child has the maturity and understanding needed to surrender through fear and pain with an open heart. It took me 30 years of groping, proving myself, and denying the fear and pain I could not yet face, before I became willing and able to do this. For all that time I was like most of my clients, living in fear and denial, avoiding the inner black hole of psychic pain we all carry within. I had no reason to face the pain, for at this time in my life I did not yet know what I would find beneath it.

Then I met a woman named Karen and fell madly, ecstatically in love. Of course, she was just as beautiful and emotionally unavailable as my mother! Not surprisingly, this relationship eventually triggered all the painful buried emotions that lost child, my earlier self, had originally suffered, emotions that had caused him to close his heart to love. Now, with Karen, I was unknowingly (and by design) re-enacting my wounding relationship with my mother in order to work through the psychic pain of my separation from love as a young child! And this is what we all do, and why each of our romantic relationships are, in reality, *a quest to find ourselves.*

And so a process began with Karen that would finally force me to surrender and fully open my heart, to let go and trust, and to eventually face and feel through the black hole of repressed anger, despair, and aloneness that I had been running from, and carrying with me my whole life. But it would be a process of difficult stages, of becoming more and more willing to keep my heart open in the face of the psychic pain that had caused me to close my heart at the age of six. And as I opened my heart and faced this pain, I finally found the wounded six-year-old boy within me who had loved so deeply and profoundly and then closed his heart when his world had seemingly collapsed.

Falling in love was a trigger for this healing process. But falling in love is no guarantee that we will achieve conscious love. As I have pointed out, a love relationship is a litmus test of our ability to love in the face of our own unhealed pain; it is a proving ground where we can, if we choose, grow from emotional love to conscious love and be healed in the process. In my case, being in love was not enough; it would take more work and courage for me to fully open my heart.

My relationship with Karen fell apart, smothered by conditional love with all its possessiveness, jealousy, and need for control. It forced me to realize that I could no longer avoid this inner child's pain. And so I finally surrendered to it completely, knowing that this pain went far deeper than losing Karen—and also knowing that Karen was *not* the source of my pain. It was *my* pain! When I took *full accountability for my pain and stopped denying love*, something wonderful happened: I spontaneously recovered the memory of that ecstatic summer day when I was four years old. I also gradually recovered many other lost, joyous childhood moments that gave fleeting glimpses and feelings of the state of soul consciousness that had marked my earliest years. And joy itself began bubbling to the surface of my consciousness. I was seeing through different eyes!

This was my first discovery that profound joy and love lay hidden *beneath* my own deepest fear and pain. At this point, at age 37, my life became truly inner, or soul-directed, as opposed to outer, or ego-directed.

I had also rediscovered the wondrous, knowing child hiding inside me, wrapped in a defensive cocoon of ego consciousness that masked his profound sadness and aloneness. It was then that I consciously began my quest to fully free that child from his self-imposed cocoon so he could truly be himself. And out of this came my life's work of connecting to the trapped child within others and facilitating their path to inner joy and freedom.

Now I clearly see my whole life as a quest to return to, live from, and share with others that joyful state of soul consciousness that we all once knew and felt as children. The ideas presented in this book are the culmination of my own life experience and of my extensive counseling experience as a licensed therapist, and are also corroborated by substantial supportive research over the last 30 years.

Having shared these truths in my work with hundreds of individuals from all walks of life over many years, I find that most people instinctively feel them to be true, for they resonate at people's deepest level of consciousness. And the central, liberating truth on which my work is based, which helps people to finally face and feel through the pain and despair that they have been running from all their lives, is this: *The deep underlying unity of the universe is a psychic energy field of love and soul consciousness that lies not only beyond time and space but also beneath our deepest fears.*

When this truth is realized, the external search is over: "It" was never "out there" to be found, but has always been within us to be surrendered to!

By "surrender," I don't mean "giving up" or "giving in to," but, rather, "letting go." The following personal story graphically illustrates what I mean by surrender. At the time, I was a Navy carrier pilot on the USS *Ranger*. It was a cold December night on the South China Sea in 1962, and I was preparing to take off in a driving rain that made the carrier deck slick and dangerous for both the plane handlers and launch crew. I quickly scanned my instruments, brought my F3H Demon to full throttle, and felt the powerful Navy supersonic jet impatiently lean against the restraining bridle. On the deck below, the launch crew chief braced himself against the biting wind sweeping the heavy rain down the deck. His neon batons raised and poised, he awaited my salute, which I gave. I then waited for his signal to the launch crew to release the bridle, a simple act that would send me hurtling into the stormy night sky.

At his signal, I braced my head against the headrest and awaited the sudden rush of acceleration. Within seconds, thousands of pounds of steam pressure drove me back into the seat and catapulted my plane forward and into the night air at 135 knots. My hands and eyes quickly swept through the cockpit as I had done hundreds of times before. I awaited my gradual acceleration to climbing speed. But it did not come. Something was wrong! I was not gaining airspeed!

My airspeed indicator was pegged at 135 knots, and the radar altimeter told me I was only 30 feet over the water. I was at 100 percent power, yet my plane was dangerously close to stalling speed and I was rapidly losing altitude. I had no idea what was wrong!

Another quick visual check of my instrument panel told me I was now only 20 feet over the water. The plane began to shudder, nearing a stall as I fought to stay airborne. In a state of total panic, I frantically reviewed what I perceived as my only options.

The first option was to take the plane into the water, hoping that I might survive the crash and be rescued. If I survived the crash, I knew I could only survive for three minutes in the freezing South China Sea. And the helicopter rescue crew was not on station because of the poor weather conditions.

The second option was to eject in my rocket seat and hope the carrier wouldn't crush me in its propeller screws. And I would still have only three minutes to survive in the icy water.

With the stall horn blaring, only seconds away from crashing, I felt myself being literally crushed into the seat by the enormity of my desperate situation. It was then that I exercised a third option: I completely let go. I totally surrendered to the feeling of being crushed into my seat in desperate fear. I'll never forget the sensation of what came next. Suddenly, I entered into the marvelous peace of absolute surrender. My mind went beyond its incredible fear and panic. I became acutely calm and clear.

I quickly scanned the cockpit again. Now I saw that the landing gear handle light was still on. I realized I had failed to raise the lever after take-off! The plane was carrying too much drag to gain airspeed and altitude. I quickly raised the gear handle and the jet immediately responded, rising from just above the icy sea and heading skyward.

Many years later I realized that the crushing feeling I had experienced that night on the South China Sea was a reliving of my original birth trauma. I also realized that I had exercised in the cockpit of that F3H Demon the same option I had exercised at my birth: I had surrendered!

Learning to surrender is what our life's journey is all about. But the journey doesn't really "take off" until we finally and fully surrender to love, "lift the lever," and go through our deepest fears and pain into the well of soul consciousness that lies even deeper within.

The worst prison is a closed heart. Yet most of us lock ourselves in that prison for much, if not all, of our lives. This prison, whose walls are constructed from fear and unworthiness, keeps us from fully experiencing love and from being who we truly are.

As I have tried to show you, it is only by fully opening our hearts and surrendering to the love that lies beneath our deepest fears and terror, that we can begin to take our place in this loving plan, and eventually sing our own unique song—by fully sharing the gift of ourselves with others.

In essence, my lifetime quest to find myself has been a process of learning to surrender to what was already deepest within myself and then finding the courage to fully share what I truly felt and knew. That is how I sing my song as I'm singing it now with you. My purpose in writing this book is to *ignite* your personal quest to heal yourself; to show you how you, too, can fully surrender to the love that is deepest within yourself; and to inspire *you* to ignite others by fully opening your heart and showing up in life as the unique and loving person you really are.

If you do this, you will be giving the world the greatest gift of all—*the gift of yourself!*

4

the
three tenets
of the
Unified
Field

The Unified Field of love, or soul consciousness, is accessed through your willingness to surrender to it. Owning and integrating the Field requires all of your courage, as well as a deep and abiding faith in yourself. The initial phase of this work involves surrendering to the lonely, wounded child within and rediscovering the truths he or she once knew. Next comes a process of learning to stand alone in this discovery—to become inner-directed, or to develop what I call *inner validation*. By engaging this ongoing process with great intention, one enters a state of soul consciousness, or a conscious connection to the Unified Field.

When you reach a place of inner direction and validation, the outer world responds through synchronistic events that are directly related to your subjective life and that are also directly proportional to your willingness to surrender and let go of the ego's need to control and protect itself. When this begins to happen to my clients, they find it incredibly exciting and scary. I humorously call this stage "being on the Express versus the Local." These experiences of serendipity are literal evidence that you are in the Field, which is beyond the limitations of time and space.

Here is a good analogy: Imagine yourself, for a moment, being a sailboat, your heart being the sails, and the wind being grace. (Grace is the universe saying "Yes!" to you.) Most people say no to themselves by keeping their hearts closed; their sails are at best halfway up and they wonder why they don't seem to be going anywhere. But when you say "Yes!" to yourself, at the risk of everything, and fully open your heart, you are no longer controlled by fear. Your sail is fully raised, and you move out of the trough of the wave onto the crest, the *Express,* and into connection with the Unified Field of love.

And yes, it's exciting and scary at times. But it's also real and authentic, versus unreal and superficial. And to the degree that you respond to this inner call to open your heart, you begin to feel the joy and peace of being part of something far greater than yourself and of knowing that you have a part to play in this loving plan.

At each step in my own process of surrendering and letting go, people have appeared, and events have occurred, offering gifts that helped me take the next step. Many friends, lovers, and clients have played a part in my healing, growth, and discovery process, as many people will play a part in yours. They taught me that standing alone and sharing my truth is really taking responsibility for my function in the loving plan. They led me to see that singing my unique song is really the same as *belonging*. And so it is with a humble and grateful heart that I share with you these core truths of the Unified Field.

What follows then are the three tenets of the Unified Field of love, which I will substantiate in the coming chapters.

Tenet One

The basic underlying force of the universe is a boundless psychic energy field of universal love within which gravitational and electromagnetic fields, subatomic realms, time, space, living things, and all other forces and aspects of nature are merely conditions of state.

Within this universal energy field of love, para-normal events such as clairvoyance, telepathy, synchro-nicity, precognition, and near-death experiences are also conditions of state. (By "conditions of state" I mean that they are inherently contained or subsumed within the Unified Field as a part of it.) The principal

property of this field of love, from the dance of subatomic particles to the planetary bodies and galaxies
hurtling and spinning in their vast orbits, is its propensity to unite, complete, and fulfill all living beings within a constantly evolving loving plan. This field of love
is the absolute constant of the universe, within which time
and space are relative conditions of state. Once we surrender to this field of love we are instantly joined with
the past, present, and future of a universe that is in a
continual process of uniting and completing itself.

Tenet Two

*The state of consciousness—or sensory
awareness—of the observer determines his
or her ability to perceive the Unified Field.*

"Sensory," as I define it, is not limited to physical
sensation but includes our awareness of every kind of
sensation or input in every dimension of our being—
physical, emotional, mental, and psychic. Any means by
which we register and experience any kind of stimulus
that impinges on our consciousness is sensory. Therefore I measure consciousness by the depth and range of
sensory experience as defined above. And there can be
no more profound sensory event than the experience
of love—through total surrender to what is deepest
within ourselves. *For what is deepest within us is love,* the
ultimate life force, a joyful state of soul consciousness
that includes and integrates all lesser states. Conversely,

the state of consciousness that limits or denies our perception of the Unified Field is ego consciousness.

Tenet Three

The pain of not feeling loved for oneself seemingly separates us from our original state of soul consciousness and breaks our childhood connection with the Unified Field. That separation is the beginning of ego consciousness. But we can reconnect with soul consciousness by going through that pain to the love and joy that lies beneath.

This pain of feeling separate or unloved is the disturbing grain of sand around which the ego coalesces. As we have seen, soul consciousness is inherently aware of, and calls us to take responsibility for, our function within the loving plan; ego consciousness *limits or denies* our perception of the Unified Field. This pain of separation from love and from our original state of soul consciousness is of such deep psychic proportions that, as I will show later, it triggers in early childhood processes in the hypothalamus that result in a left-brain dominance. This in turn increases the tendency toward denial and mistrust and the diminishing of our connection to the joy and love deepest within us. Thus we gradually descend into a dark tunnel of pain, aloneness, and despair that is a kind of spiritual or emotional death. And out of this painful death, the ego and ego consciousness are born—for survival and protection purposes only. As such, death or the idea of death, is an illusion measured by the limits of our consciousness.

The ego, in this sense, is nothing but a protective cocoon whose imprisoning dominance can gradually be shed the more we surrender to love and restore our connection to the Unified Field. *It really is this simple!*

5

Einstein was right: God doesn't play dice

Albert Einstein spent his life searching for the Unified Field, but his concept of the universe is rather remote and abstract compared with our picture of a cosmos in which one elemental field of love reigns supreme. Einstein may have uneasily sensed that light was not the sole constant of the universe at 186,284 miles per second. Indeed, the evidence of the heart shows that the universe at all levels is subject to the force of a greater constant—which I believe is the Unified Field of love. Later in this chapter we will see that Teilhard de Chardin knew this central truth and that the great psychologist Carl Jung also touched upon it.

Einstein discovered only what it was possible to

see using the limiting and dissociative scientific perspective. Science usually blinds one eye by rigidly excluding and discounting most sensory and subjective experience—or what I call *the within of things*. For example: Any scientist can freely discuss the energy of physical phenomena, but what scientist dares to propose that the essence of energy is love, even though his deepest intuition tells him this is the case? Given the current state of the scientific method, the important sensory or subjective perceptions of the observer are amputated from the scientific process. And the possibility of a subjective life existing within the things observed, from atoms to galaxies, is also dismissed. Thus Albert Einstein, a scientist bound by the prejudices of his profession, to some degree must have excluded, denied, or repressed the evidence of his own perceptions and experiences in the psychic or spiritual realm in his search for the Unified Field. And as we will see, he also denied the possibility of the inner life of the "things" which he observed, evidence for which was available in his own research into the behavior of light at the subatomic level.

Consider the so-called *photoelectric effect,* one of Einstein's key discoveries. In 1905 Einstein deduced, and then proved, that light is not a continuous stream of energy but is composed of individual particles or bundles of energy, which he named *photons.* His revolutionary explanation of the nature of light soon led others to formulate equally revolutionary theories, chief among them quantum physics.

The problem, at least from Einstein's point of view, was that quantum theory now replaced the sanctity of cause and effect with a sea of statistical probabilities. Then along came along another objectionable theory, from Einstein's viewpoint: Werner Heisenberg's now-famous Uncertainty Principle, which posited that certain aspects of reality are in principle unknowable.[1]

These bold, new proposals went deeply against Einstein's basic beliefs about the universe. "The most incomprehensible thing about the universe is its comprehensibility," he once said. And, more famously—in response to the claims of quantum theory—Einstein replied to his colleagues: "God may be subtle, but he does not play dice."[2]

But there was another rub. To explain the odd behavior of atoms and light, Einstein was forced to use current statistical theory, which he detested for the same reason that he disliked quantum mechanics: both assume that everything happens by chance, and there is no direct relationship between cause and effect. Einstein could not accept the statistical formulations of quantum mechanics as a valid basis for explaining the laws of physics. "Even the great initial success of quantum theory," he declared, "does not make me believe in the fundamental dice game."[3]

As a result, he left the quantum field to others and spent his last years searching for the elusive Unified Field theory, which he believed would be based on something other than quantum theory. To Einstein, a universe that did not run according to strict rules of cause and effect, which he hoped to discover, was totally unacceptable. He believed to the end that some logical, unifying principle or order lay hidden beneath the seemingly random behavior of atoms and photons. And he was right!

But even though he had stumbled upon the evidence of this hidden order, he never found it. And he fell far short of formulating a Unified Field theory before his death.

There are important clues as to why Einstein, with his formidable mind, could never quite grasp the Unified Field as a universal field of love. He once wrote: "I believe in Spinoza's God, who reveals himself in the harmony of what exists, not in a God who concerns himself with the fact and actions of human beings."[4] Locked in his scientific perspective, Einstein was interested in the evidence of harmony among external, physical things—the *without* of things, of heavenly bodies, large and small, moving in relation to each other. But he could not fully grasp the *within* of things. As we will see, even photons and molecules and planets contain an internal urge to attract and unite.

This problem is clearly seen in Einstein's work with the Indian physicist S.N. Bose in the early 1920s when they laid the groundwork for the later development of the laser.[5] Their findings pointed toward a Unified Field of love—yet they were unable to perceive it.

In 1925, Einstein received a paper from Bose that described light as a gas consisting of photons. The important finding in this paper was that photons do not obey the common-sense statistical laws that billiard balls do. For example, if you randomly roll a number of perfectly elastic billiard balls on a frictionless table, sooner or later they will all end up in various pockets. Photons do not. Photons, in the billiard ball scenario, will have a tendency to gather into whatever pocket the first photon falls. And the more photons in a pocket, the more likely the other photons will choose to join their mates!

Yet what did Einstein deduce from this effect? *That there was no force or attraction involved!* Instead, he posited a strange, almost "spooky" tendency that caused photons to prefer to travel together. (Einstein was fond of calling events he did not understand "spooky.") Here we must acknowledge the second tenet: that the discovery and formulation of the "laws" of physics are subjective, observer-dependent, and to some degree determined by prejudices or preconceptions we may not even be aware of. In the above case, Einstein drew a "scientific" conclusion based on an already existing mind-set.

To further test this finding, Einstein used his mathematical formulations to predict the behavior of large groups of atoms full of excess energy and with the potential to emit a photon. He wanted to see what would happen if a stray photon passed by the atom group. Lo and behold, he found that a stray photon not only stimulated the atoms to release their photons earlier than expected, but that the emitted photons then went in the same direction and at exactly the same frequency as the original, stray photon! (Spooky, huh?) All it took for someone to later invent the laser was to find a means to help the emissions along.

My point is that *Einstein and Bose actually discovered evidence of the Unified Field of love, with its innate urge to unite operating at the subatomic level.* But the obvious indicator of the presence of this field, revealed in the attractive urge of photons to unite, did not fit their prior assumptions or their level of consciousness. So they posited an unexplained tendency of photons to travel together, with no attractive force involved. (They might as well have said that all photons just *happen* to be going in the same direction.)

Now, from the standpoint of a Unified Field of love, the propensity of photons to unite is direct evidence of the universal force of love operating at the deepest micro level of the physical realm. By the same token, psi experiences, near-death experiences, synchronicity, and other phenomena that transcend time/space limitations, are in their own way evidence of the presence of the Unified Field operating at the psychic level.

In other words, Bose and Einstein discovered evidence of a primordial urge to unite existing even within the subatomic particles of energy that make up light, but they were blinded to the implications of their discovery by "scientific" prejudice.

Picture, if you will, some gigantic scientist peering through his trusty microscope at you and your lover—

someone you have chosen to spend your life with—and dismissing your deep soul connection and union as a mere "spooky tendency" to want to travel together. Has this scientist seen the full picture of you? Or has he missed an important subjective part of the picture? And if so, was there a glitch in his microscope, or were his perceptions limited because of his preconceived beliefs or his state of consciousness?

Clearly, our beliefs and level of consciousness as observers determines our ability to accurately comprehend what we observe. It also determines the degree to which we consciously experience the Unified Field of love. As the William James analogy that ended Chapter 2 implies, an open heart is as important for accurate scientific inquiry as is a powerful microscope—if not more important. Science will surely remain one-eyed and lacking in depth-perception until it acknowledges the equal validity of subjective, sensory, and spiritual experience. And it will continue to record the letter of mere mechanics, and miss the true spirit that brings it all to life, until it comes to recognize the universal urge to unite—even within the molecule itself—as being the universal attractive force of love.

No one describes this scientific impasse more tellingly than Lincoln Barnett, author of *The Universe and Dr. Einstein:* "A theoretical concept is emptied of content to the degree that it is divorced from sensory experience, for the only world man can truly know is the world created for him by his senses. Beyond that point he stares into the void."[6]

In his many books, Teilhard de Chardin provided the needed bridge between this void and the truest sensory perception of love:

> What name should we give . . . [to that] to which all activities displayed by the stuff of the universe are finally reduced? Only one name is possible: love. The physical structure of the universe is love.[7]

Unlike Einstein, Teilhard clearly grasped the fact that the attractive force of love must necessarily rule at the atomic level of the universe or else love could not appear at higher levels. "If there were no real propensity to unite . . . indeed, in the molecule itself," he wrote, "it would be physically impossible for love to appear higher up in 'hominized' form."

Thus, where Einstein was more concerned with the without of things, Teilhard was primarily concerned in his writings with the within of things. Teilhard used the term "within" to denote the psychic face or consciousness of matter which, since the beginning of time, has revealed itself in its urge to unite.

Teilhard defines this inner urge as an energy force in his famous *law of complexity-consciousness.* The law states two principles:

> 1. Throughout all time there has been an evolutionary tendency for all matter to unite and become increasingly complex in nature.

2. With each increase in material complexity, there is a related rise in the consciousness of matter, and an even greater urge to unite.[8]

Teilhard divided this fundamental energy into two distinct components: a tangential energy that links any element with all others of the same order; and a radial energy that represents the innate urge toward union, greater complexity, and what he called *leaps in consciousness.* For example, we are all tangentially linked to one another because we are classed as human beings. But we are all radially linked to one another by a common urge (however well disguised by fear) to unite with one another—an urge inherent in the very molecules of which we are composed.

This radial energy in matter; the deep and universal urge toward union, complexity, and increasing awareness, ultimately manifests itself as *conscious* love. And the primal energetic manifestation of love that permeates the cosmos is the very fabric of the Unified Field. In other words, Teilhard's concept of radial energy is both a state of soul consciousness and also the Unified Field itself.

But let's briefly move from the microcosm to the macrocosm and apply Teilhard's law of complexity-consciousness to the established theories of evolution and the Big Bang.

Consider the fact that each progressive stage of evolution must result in greater complexity and consciousness and also accelerates evolution itself. Put another way, time and evolution speed up in direct proportion to our increased capacity to love. Thus Earth's Precambrian period, in which the first highly organized nucleated cells were evolving in the primordial sea, encompasses some seven-eighths of our planet's entire history of 4.6 billion years. It took nearly four billion years for the first amphibian to crawl out of the sea onto dry land. But as evolution began to accelerate, and because of the innate urge to unite, it required just a few hundred thousand years for the first upright man to finally walk on the moon.

In the light of the Unified Field theory, it would seem that love (or spirit) is the irreducible and motivating force of the universe. This is the fundamental implication of my Unified Field theory: that from the prehistoric depths of the primordial sea to the present age of 'hominized' man, *life unfolds in a seemingly endless evolution within a conscious loving plan.*

Again, Teilhard sums it up most eloquently when he writes, "Driven by the forces of love, the fragments of the world seek each other so that the world may come to being."[9]

Thus humankind is a key phase in the evolution of love. It is part of an ongoing energy transformation of life into forms that are ever more complex, more conscious, and more loving. We human beings are literally the cutting-edge product (as far as we know) of an evolution of love!

Consider this: In the August 1990 issue of *Life* magazine,[10] photographer Lennart Nilsson captured the miracle of creation with unprecedented pictures of

Two separate nuclei containing chromosomes from the male sperm and the female ovum unite to form a single nucleus that will eventually become a new human being.

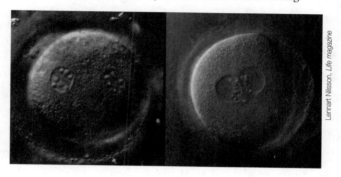

Lennart Nilsson, *Life magazine*

how human life begins. His photographs of human conception, from its first moment through its earliest hours and days, offer dramatic proof of life's primal urge to unite and of Teilhard's law of complexity-consciousness.

These incredible photographs reveal a remarkable sequence of events: First, the head of the sperm enters the ovum (having raced there like a bee to honey). There, two small chromosome-filled bubbles—one from the man and one from the woman—float in orbit around each other. Drawn inexorably together, these nuclei begin to unite. The result of this union is a single, highly complex nucleus containing the entire biological blueprint for a human being.

About 12 hours later, this complex cell splits into two. Then these two cells divide again, and so on, and finally produce a new, far more complex and conscious nucleus called a blastocyst, composed of more than a hundred cells. Evolving continually, the blastocyst begins its journey through the fallopian tube toward the uterus. Once there, it attaches itself to the uterine wall and signals to the woman that she is pregnant. By the third trimester, this prenatal child—in a perfect demonstration of the Teilhardian process of complexity-consciousness—has evolved into a fully developed hu-man infant, floating in an amniotic and blissful state of soul consciousness.

Intriguing evidence of prenatal soul consciousness was discovered by Dr. William Emerson of Petaluma, California, in the 1970s. Emerson evaluated the memory and consciousness capacities of the prenatal child through regressions of 75 children ages two to four. A variety of regressive techniques were utilized, and these young children were asked to be aware of any images, symbols, thoughts, feelings, sensations, visions, and so forth that emerged. They were also reminded that nothing at all might emerge, and that this was also quite normal and all right.

To determine whether the material obtained through these regressions pointed to genuine experiences of prenatal higher consciousness, the children's experiences were evaluated using four criteria. These criteria, which were selected by examining phenomenological reports of higher consciousness by adults, were as follows:

1. Did the experiences contain documented symbols of higher consciousness or divine consciousness?

2. Did the experiences contain positive elements of higher consciousness, such as ecstasy, joy, or bliss?

3. Was there evidence of fetal omniscience (knowledge of events that seemed to transcend the sensory and mental capacities of the fetus)?

4. Was there evidence of higher learning (learning that demonstrated a depth of understanding and wisdom)?

The results of the regressions revealed that most of the children's experiences met two of the four criteria and that many met three of the four.[11] These results support my belief that our earliest experience—in this case, prenatal life—is marked by states of soul consciousness that imply our fundamental connection to a Unified Field of love.

This field of love—whose principal urge to unite affects all matter, from individual particles of light to slow-wheeling galaxies, to every child conceived in every womb—is the ontological matrix within which my psychological work with others is done. And its initial acceptance, which finally leads to the direct experience of this living matrix that I call the Unified Field of love, is what gives my work its healing and transformative power.

And consider this: Each complex and conscious cell in our body is animated by (and perhaps even feels and responds to) a universal urge to unite. If this urge is indeed love, then love is literally the attractive force that unites all atoms, molecules, and cells of which everything is made, including ourselves; love is the very force that holds our bodies together. And we humans, being the most complex and conscious form of matter that we know of, must have a correspondingly greater capacity and need to unite with and love one another than mere atoms, molecules, and cells do. So consider how painful and confusing it must be, and in fact is, when we resist and deny this primal, universal urge to love.

Why do we resist? Because this primal urge to unite is overridden by our fears and by the state of fear-based ego consciousness in which we tend to live. Then how do we overcome our fears? By surrendering through them to the joy, love, and soul consciousness that lies beneath in the very source of our being—in the Unified Field of love.

Within this evolution of love on earth, the human species is being called to surrender beyond its limited ego consciousness and take full responsibility for this urge to love, unite, and cooperate. But this can only happen when enough *individuals* take such responsibility and when, by doing so, they are able to heal and grow into their soul-conscious connection to the Unified Field of love.

Along these same lines, Carl Jung has written:

We are, in the deepest sense, the victims and the instruments of cosmogonic love. I do not use love in its connotations of desiring, preferring, favoring, wishing, and similar feelings, but as something superior to the individual—a unified and undivided whole.[12]

Jung's theories of the collective unconscious fit within and support the model of a Unified Field of love as a universal psychic energy field that unites and interconnects all beings. In *Religion and the Collective Unconscious*, June Singer explains:

> The collective unconscious, as Jung perceived it, does not merely derive from personal experience but precedes the individual in time. It is not individual, but universal, carrying traces of the entire evolution of the species. Thus, the collective unconscious is a principle identical in all men and constitutes a substratum of a suprapersonal nature which is in all human beings.[13]

As such, the Unified Field, like the collective unconscious, is a boundless psychic energy field that precedes us in time. You might say that both exist within us, yet we are born into them. But the suprapersonal substratum of the Unified field is *love*. Love is a universal urge that carries within itself the traces of the entire evolution of the species in terms of its urge to unite and complete itself. Indeed, love does constitute a substratum of a suprapersonal nature that is present in all human beings. Even Jung's theory of synchronicity (meaningful coincidences) can be explained as the working out of our *individual yet interconnected* destinies within a unified psychic energy field of love within an evolving loving plan.

Jung was convinced that deep within the unconscious—in the hidden regions of the human psyche
that profoundly influence the conscious mind—lay all
the answers for the unfolding and perfection of each
human being. He was also convinced that a source of
energy, a psychic equivalent to that released by the
splitting of the atom, could be released from the psyche's hidden depths. And he was correct! The primal
force of love, the universal urge to unite and create ever
more complex and conscious forms, *is* that energy!

Both Jung and Einstein intuited the existence
of an underlying and unifying field, with its own set
of laws and principles that united the universe into a
single and undivided whole. Einstein searched for that
field within the universe of matter (and note how
astronomers have documented the "urge to unite" on
a galactic scale—see adjacent photo). Jung also found
evidence of it within the deepest regions of the human
psyche. Teilhard experienced it with his illumined
heart. And I verified it by my willingness to fully love
and surrender through my darkest fears to what was
deepest within myself.

Now you, by choosing to love and surrender
through your worst fears to what is deepest within
yourself, can also discover and directly experience the
Unified Field that many of the greatest scientific minds
of our age have missed. In the process you too will
discover that love is indeed the threshold to another
universe—and to a new way of being!

Photo taken by the Hubble Space Telescope captures
galaxies being drawn to unite with each other in clusters.

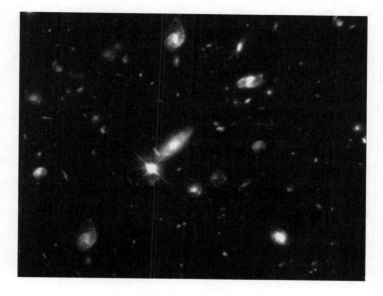

6

understanding the near- and after-death experience

Teilhard de Chardin's lifework was the reinterpretation of Christianity in the light of evolution, but his great life problem was that few people could see or feel the truths that were so obvious to him. Teilhard knew what lay beyond death decades before the well-documented wave of near-death experiences that has became a modern-day phenomenon. He yearned for some sign or signal to be given from beyond so that others might know what he knew. In this vein, he wrote:

> How comforting and 'electrifying' it would be if some signal or sign, some summons or echo, should come to us from beyond death and give us positive assurance that some center of convergence really does exist ahead of us.[1]

Today, we seem to be receiving countless such "electrifying" signals. Tens of thousands of reported near-death experiences in the past few decades, with their defining effects of peace, unity, clarity, light, and joy, point explicitly to a "center of convergence." This center of convergence lies beyond death (and perhaps before birth), and, I believe, within each of us as a state of soul consciousness. The late Dr. Elisabeth Kubler-Ross, the internationally respected expert on the psychiatric dimensions of dying, pioneered in this field with her claim to have proof that "there is life after death"—on the basis of hundreds of near-death experiencers whom she had personally interviewed. Early in her work in a 1975 interview she explained her findings:

> I have investigated cases from Australia to California, involving patients from age 2 to 96. I have hundreds of very clear-cut cases from all over the world, both religious and nonreligious people—one had even been dead 12½ hours. All experienced the same thing. They virtually shed their physical bodies, as a butterfly comes out of the cocoon.
>
> They describe a feeling of peace, often beautiful, indescribable peace—no pain, no anxiety—and they experienced themselves as perfect, completely whole. After the transition (following death) you achieve a higher understanding which includes a review of your own life. You evaluate all your actions, words, and thoughts; you are fully aware of the effects of your deeds and thoughts on others. It is not God who condemns you; you condemn yourself.[2]

Startling evidence of signs reaching us from beyond death came in a 1988 article in the *Noetic Sciences Review*. Journalist Andrew Greeley reported that nearly half of all American adults believed that they had been in contact with someone who had died, usually a spouse or sibling. One significant aspect of these "close encounters" was the respondents' belief in a loving God rather than a judgmental one.[3] (How can there be a Unified Field of love *and* an angry, judgmental God?)

In the intervening years, a host of near-death researchers (some of them near-death experiencers themselves) weighed in with equally significant findings. Raymond Moody, P.M.H. Atwater, Kenneth Ring, Danion Brinkley, and others interviewed many thousands of near-death experiencers, whose accounts overwhelmingly corroborated the conclusions of Kubler-Ross's pioneering work. The testimony of these individuals of every age and from every walk of life—not to mention findings that 40 percent of Americans report having had mystical or "peak" experiences—supports the idea that we are all inherently linked to a Unified Field of love and that the experience of this field coincides with a psychic state of soul consciousness that is profoundly life-altering.[4]

While in the timeless state of soul consciousness, most of these individuals encounter, according to Dr. Moody, a deeply loving, nonjudgmental spirit of brilliant light.[5] They become aware that they have a function or spiritual purpose within a loving plan, and they recognize whether or not they have fulfilled it. Other commonly reported experiences are of moving rapidly through a long dark tunnel to a place of light; feelings of oneness with all; no sense of time and space; and profound feelings of peace and of being unconditionally loved.

P. M. H. Atwater, in her book *Beyond the Light: What Isn't Being Said about Near-Death Experiences,* describes other commonly reported feelings that seem to be inherent in these experiences:

> Theirs is the thrill of being engulfed in total, overwhelming love beyond precedent, beyond description, a feeling of oneness and worth, of total freedom and acceptance. No stipulations, conditions, or criteria, just boundless, infinite, all-encompassing love, so forgiving, so total, so immense that nothing can contain it. . . . They lose all fear of death, for they know it ends nothing but the physical body and its facade of personality.[6]

Atwater also reports a typical sense of mission or purpose that lingers, like an after-effect, in those who have returned from this state of bliss:

> What keeps us here is a knowledge that we have more to learn, a job to do or a task yet to perform—and that somehow we must get on with it.

> Our sense of mission is coupled with the awareness of our integral part in a divine or greater plan—no matter how mundane or insignificant our parts may be.[7]

Perhaps the most vivid description of the Unified

Field and the egoless state of soul consciousness is the account of the near-death experience of Victor Solow, a 56-year-old New York filmmaker and religious skeptic, who was dead for 23 minutes before being revived by a team of doctors.

Here is Solow's description of what happened "over there":

> I was moving at great speed toward a net or grid of great luminosity. The instant I made contact with it, the vibrant luminosity increased to a blinding intensity which drained, absorbed, and transformed me at the same time. There was no pain. The sensation was neither pleasant nor unpleasant but completely consuming. Now I was not in a place, nor even a dimension, but rather in a condition of being.

> This new "I" was not the "I" which I knew, but rather a distilled essence of it . . . something vaguely familiar, something I had always known which had been buried under a superstructure of personal fears, hopes, wants, and needs. This "I" had no connection to ego.

> It was final, unchangeable, indivisible, indestructible pure spirit.

> While completely unique and as individual as a fingerprint, "I" was, at the same time, part of some infinite, harmonious, and ordered whole. I had been there before . . . .[8]

The new "I" that Solow describes is the pure state of the true self previously buried under the ego's superstructure of personal fears, hopes, wants, and needs. This "I," unique and yet universal, is part of an infinite and harmonious whole—the Unified Field of love.

Note Solow's description of the Unified Field as a "net or grid of great luminosity" joining all living beings within its energy field of love. We also saw Longfellow describe this all-encompassing net as "The thread of all sustaining beauty that runs through all and doth all unite."[9]

It is also remarkable how this image of the "net" parallels the superstring theory of modern physics. Superstring theory posits a universe of strings, one-dimensional vibrating loops a billionth of a trillionth of an inch long, underlying all forces and matter. It provides a framework for understanding all known particles and forces of nature, uniting them in a single context or matrix. As vibrating guitar strings can cause other nearby strings to resonate, the "super" strings of superstring theory *all vibrate and interact with one another.*[10] And what, pray tell, are they vibrating with? Why *love*! (Did you really need to ask?)

The phenomena associated with near-death experiences indicate a state of soul consciousness within us all, hidden beneath our typical state of ego consciousness. Yet we don't have to die, or even almost die, to return to this state; for my work with hundreds of clients during the past 25 years has shown me that one need not have a near-death experience in order to experience soul consciousness! Through deeply surrendering to love, we can pass voluntarily through the birthplace of the ego—that black tunnel of psychic pain hidden within each of us—and return to our original state of soul consciousness and our innate connection to the Unified Field.

Modern physics has shown that the consciousness of the observer determines what is seen or experienced; modern psychology has shown that what we see "outside" is a reflection of what is inside. Accordingly, when we surrender to our propensity to love and unite with all, we will see that *the entire universe itself has always been loving and uniting with all!* But we can't see this love in the universe surrounding us until we find it in ourselves.

Carl Jung knew this truth profoundly. In his work regarding the *shadow* and the phenomenon of *projection*, he showed how our fear and terror of the unknowns of the universe—whether bogeymen under the bed, commies in Hollywood, or devouring black holes in space—are reflections of the fear and terror we have not yet faced within ourselves. An amusing Indian aphorism makes the same point: "If a pickpocket is in a crowd of saints, all he sees are pockets."

It's not surprising that our lives are so inextricably bound with archetypal images of terror which we then project onto the world around us. For our entry into life is a traumatic passage through a black tunnel of fear, an experience of being inescapably drawn into and swallowed by a terrifying black hole that pulls us into another world! The birth process itself evokes parallels with the near-death experience.

Picture yourself for a moment being drawn into a black hole in space and helplessly crushed by a force far greater than yourself. Would it feel something like the following account?

> An intransigent force—wild, out of control—
> has gripped the infant.
> A blind force that hammers at it and impels it
> downward. . . .
>
> Overpowered, it huddles up as tightly as it can. . . .
>
> The walls close in further still. The cell becomes a
> passageway; the passage, a tunnel.
> With its heart bursting, the infant sinks into this hell.
> Its fear is without limit. . . .
>
> Then everything explodes!
> The whole world bursts open.
> No more tunnel, no prison, no monster.
> The child is born.[11]

These are the words of Frederick Leboyer, the famous French pediatrician, describing the birth trauma. Birth and death both represent archetypal passages from one state, or world, to another—and are therefore universally apt metaphors for spiritual and psychological transformation.[12]

These metaphors also guide my own life process and my psychological work with clients in their transition from ego consciousness to soul consciousness.

For example, both my original birth trauma and my carrier pilot experience over the South China Sea were life-or-death situations dealing with forces and events that seemed totally beyond my control. Both times I fully experienced and finally surrendered to crushing sensations and overwhelming terror. When I surrendered, I discovered a hidden source of strength or consciousness guiding me through my fear and over to the "other side." As a result, I am alive today (not on the bottom of the South China Sea) and I know the state of soul consciousness. This level of consciousness beneath our deepest fears is the ultimate guide and source of strength that awaits us all.

I am a licensed therapist with well over 10,000 hours of experience dealing with people's deepest fears, terrors, and anxieties. I can unequivocally state that surrendering to long-repressed feelings of pain and despair is almost always experienced subjectively as a dark, never-ending tunnel leading only to death—and clinical practice demonstrates that people will tend to avoid such an encounter at all costs. For it is in truth a re-experiencing both of our original birth trauma and of our later, anguished separation from soul consciousness in childhood.

Surrendering to these feelings is truly like a death process.

Time after time, people have told me from the depths of that despair that the pain they are experiencing will never end, that they will never get out of that tunnel, and that they will surely die. However, it is the ego and our fears that die when we fully surrender to love and go through this experience. And when we do this, we eventually come out on the "other side" into a new life, a new way of being.

So the great surrender is also a like a *birth* process.

I prefer to call it transmutation, for we are being transformed from one kind of being into another. Love is the vehicle for this passage.

Indeed, the butterfly of the authentic person has finally emerged from its cocoon.

The great physicist Steven Hawking has suggested that black holes may become white holes at a point of singularity. Similarly, near-death experiencers report a light at the end of a dark tunnel, while our birth through the "dark tunnel" of the womb delivers us to the light of this world. I am suggesting that at the end of the black hole of despair within us we reach a point of *psychic* singularity. In this place, all notions of time and space break down; we experience a reversal in the polarity of our being; and we re-establish our conscious connection with the Unified Field as we return to our original state of soul consciousness.

In other words, the singularity at the center of a black hole, where time and space come to an end, parallels the singularity within each of us that leads us from darkness and despair into the brilliant light of the Unified Field that is the ground of our being. I would argue that the force that pulls us through is love, a force so strong that all conscious beings will eventually have to surrender to its lure.

This center within each of us to which we are drawn is much like Teilhard's famous "omega":

> It is necessary and sufficient for us that we should extend our science to its farthest limits and recognize and accept . . . the radiation as a present reality of that mysterious center of our centers which I have called omega.[13]

What then is the meaning of this journey that seemingly begins with birth, moves through life, and ends in death? Death has been called the raising of the final curtain, the parting of the final veil. But why wait for the final curtain to fall in order to understand who we are and why we are here? We can raise the curtain now by fully surrendering to love by passing through the tunnel of our deepest fears and pain and entering a state of soul consciousness, the "electrifying sign" at our core. As such, we will pass through the black hole within ourselves and reach the light on the other side—the light of the Unified Field that is always shining in our hidden depths.

Let me conclude by telling one more dramatic story of a near-death experiencer. Not long ago I was interviewed by the CBS-TV affiliate in San Francisco on the meaning of the near-death experience.[14] I was asked to comment on film footage of an experiencer named Terry Meyers. A few days later CBS received this note from Terry:

> Eight years ago I had a spiritual rebirth. A virus literally destroyed my heart in a matter of four days. While at the hospital, when my heart stopped, I had a near-death experience. After coming back to life, I was overwhelmed with an intense feeling of joy and love.
>
> Everything was clear to me—my purpose in life and why this happened to me. I fully understood how everything in the universe is evolved around love and my deep need to be a part of it—and today my desire to help others is driven by this passion!
>
> Dr. Allen Roland's television interview validated all the feelings I had experienced like no one else has been able to do. It is as though he had looked into my soul and mind and was speaking my thoughts.

Here's as pure a description of the transmutation as any—but again, this kind of breakthrough is available to you *right now.* We can reach those shining depths if we stop being controlled by fear, open our hearts, and begin to trust and express our deepest feelings. For they will finally lead us to the joy that lives at our core. This is the work required of us if we are to evolve as human beings.

And that is what this book will help you do.

7

beneath the well of grief is a spring of joy

Those who would not slip beneath
the still surface on the well of grief
Turning downward through its black water
to the place we cannot breathe
will never know the source from which we drink
the secret water, cold and clear
nor find in the darkness glimmering
the small round coins
thrown by those who wished for
something else.

—David Whyte

I have drawn parallels between the image of a tunnel commonly associated with near-death experiences, and the idea of a psychic tunnel of despair—

or what I call the *well of grief*—that most of us carry within us from childhood. This well of grief can also be likened to an emotional "black hole" that we feel we must avoid at all costs and which tragically separates us from the spring of joy that lies beneath it. I have also shown how we first enter this tunnel in childhood when we reluctantly and painfully shift from our original state of soul consciousness to a separated cocoon of ego consciousness which, like all cocoons, is eventually meant to be shed.

In this chapter we will examine more closely how we cocoon away our authentic selves in childhood in the unconscious belief that being ourselves is not enough. We'll discuss the effect of this separation from love on all levels of our health.

We'll also consider how we, as young children, create an ego in order to survive what is, in effect, a tragic no-win situation—*for children have no option but to choose to become a false self.* They must do this to avoid feeling the pain of the rejection of who they really are. Indeed, to somehow get the love they crave, young children are forced to cut themselves off from soul consciousness. Strong evidence points to the fact that dislocations actually occur in the brain that reinforce this pattern of separation from self and others.

This psychic pain of feeling unloved for who we really are—the fate of most children in our culture— is without doubt the most devastating of all human experiences. This childhood dilemma is particularly tragic when we bear in mind that children originally come from a place of such immense love!

As such, children have no choice but to avoid the feelings associated with this excruciating pain of rejection. As a result, we all, at some point in our early childhood, abandon our authentic feelings and create a false self through painstaking trial and error. We do this for a very good reason: we perform this emotional disconnect on ourselves to become acceptable to others, to survive psychologically, and because of our ongoing fear of losing love. As young children we are not aware of doing this. And yet this separation from love profoundly affects our being on every level—physical, emotional, mental, and spiritual.

The health impact of this loss is measurable in many ways. The advent of the science of mind–body medicine in recent times has been a blessing in that it provides clear documentation of the effects of the loss of love on our health.

The scientific evidence goes all the way back to the 1940s. For example, Dr. James J. Lynch, in his classic, *The Broken Heart: the Medical Consequences of Loneliness,* cites an early study at Cornell Medical School on the effect of sudden severe interpersonal events, such as the loss of a loved one, on the human heart. In this 1949 study, four doctors examined 12 unselected patients who had previously had cardiac difficulties and who had come to the hospital complaining of chest palpitation. They took exhaustive life histories on each and interviewed them repeatedly. "All had experienced the lack of parental love in childhood, had not married, had encountered serious marital problems, or were divorced," the study indicated. "In every case, the onset of the patient's cardiac problems could be traced to a specific traumatic interpersonal event in the patient's life."[1]

Another early study that is cited by Lynch, this time conducted at Cincinnati General Hospital, found that in 24 of 25 consecutive cases of congestive heart failure examined, the onset of the crisis had been precipitated by severe emotional stress. Of even greater interest is the list of causes they found that had precipitated the emotional stress, such as sudden death of a son, desertion by a wife, and rejection by a husband. "The emotional events all seemed to involve the loss of some type of human love or the loss of security gained from human contact. The lack of love or sudden loss of love, they pointed out, acted like 'the straw that broke the camel's back.'"[2]

In this landmark book, Dr. Lynch concluded that "there is reflected in our hearts a biological basis to form loving human relationships. If we fail to fulfill that need, our health is in peril." [3]

Since that time, numerous well-designed studies have demonstrated a clear link between love and health in adults; many others have shown a link between lack of love and diminished physical, mental, and emotional development in young children. Most recently, Dr. Dean Ornish—who is internationally recognized for showing the impact of diet and lifestyle on heart disease—summarized the results of the best scientific studies, citing experiments involving hundreds of thousands of people around the world that show the healing power of love. In his very important book, *Love & Survival: 8 Pathways to Intimacy and Health,* Ornish declares that no other factor has a greater impact on our health than love and intimacy.[4]

These studies support my argument that our childhood separation from the source of love, or soul consciousness, is the event from which springs most of our future suffering—in our health, in our relationships, and in our psychological and emotional lives.

Further, these studies implicitly support my contention that our return to the source of love, to our conscious connection with the Unified Field itself, is a decisive event that allows us to heal and to achieve a level of emotional and psychological wholeness that is not attainable by any other means.

My own direct observation has also proved to my satisfaction the link between love and health. In 1977 and 1978, I conducted a nonfunded research project called the Chrysalis Project under the direction of Dr. Roger Snyder with the cooperation of the Sonoma County Medical Association.[5] The purpose of this study was to investigate the role of self-directed beliefs and emotions on the onset, development, and outcome of cancer and other life-threatening illnesses. (By self-directed I mean beliefs and feelings people hold about themselves such as, "I'm a loser" or "I don't have what it takes" or "I'm no good, not worthy of being loved.") The 15 people involved in the study (13 had cancer and the other two severe colitis) represented a true random population. No attempt was made to screen patients according to their childhood pathology, type of illness, or onset of illness.

When the results came in, all 15 subjects indicated the belief that a significant amount of unresolved stress from childhood had played an important role in their illness. Thirteen of them believed that the onset of the illness was directly related to the loss or threatened loss of a major love relationship. The remaining two believed that their illness was directly related to deep guilt feelings that were tied to a major relationship.

There was an interesting correlation in this study between the expression and sharing of self-directed beliefs and emotions, and a positive improvement or remission of the illness. I also was able to document a link between a strong ego defense—with its characteristic rigidity and emotional repression of feelings—and a resultant deterioration or metastasizing of the illness.

I observed that the cancer patients whose condition deteriorated did not see themselves as connected to a whole but rather held onto their deep feelings of aloneness and emotional isolation. I concluded that the energy used for ego defense (protection from psychic and interpersonal pain) impairs the natural immunological system of the body, increasing the chances that abnormal cell growth and other health disorders may occur. I believe that ego defenses do this by effectively separating us from ourselves and others, and thus from our connection to love. Love, the primal energy of life, is the greatest healing force there is. Without love, radiant health and full aliveness are not possible.

As we have seen, strong evidence suggests that separation from love can lead to illness, death, or self-destructive actions. Separating from the Unified Field of love begins in our earliest childhood, in our most primary relationships with caregivers who are themselves profoundly separated from love and their own authentic feelings.

The pioneering psychologist Arthur Janov vividly communicates this tragic yet commonplace scenario in his classic, *The Feeling Child*:

> Actions and interactions between parent and child are only important insofar as they reflect feeling. Loving a child should be as natural as breathing air. Children take both for granted, but when love is missing there is a frantic and usually unconscious struggle. Imagine the desperation, the panic, the unbearable pain that would occur if breathable air were suddenly not there. It is no different for an infant or a child when love is not there.
>
> Love, as primally defined, is necessary for life.[6]

My observation, from my own experience and my work with my clients, is that the ego is born from this no-choice situation as a means of surviving the loss or the threatened loss of love.

Like most of you, I too experienced such a no-choice dilemma as a child: My option was either to somehow re-experience the excruciating repressed emotions of my separation from love, or, to cut myself off from my true self in order to survive. I seemingly had no choice but to separate from who I really was. But it was still my choice; I was not ready to face my own well of grief!

I can still remember standing in the hall of my stepfather's house at age six, suddenly realizing I would never again see my grandfather—the person who had been the main source of love in my life. I vividly remember feeling complete panic and desperation, feeling utterly alone and full of hopeless despair.

I remember when my grandfather eventually came to visit and how I refused to go out on the back porch to see him. I could not bear to face the repressed emotions of the original traumatic event that would be triggered by his leaving again. My heart had closed to block out these unbearable feelings. Emotionally, I had stopped growing.

It was as if I had been separated from love, when in fact I had separated *myself* from love by closing my heart to avoid feeling pain. Soon after, I began frantically acting out to avoid these feelings. I stole, lied, set fires, and even contracted asthma. No one recognized my desperate cries for help. Finally, to win the love and approval I desperately longed for, convinced that being myself was not enough, I made a decision to become just like my older brother. I developed a persona, a false self, patterned after him. That was when my ego crystallized. I later grew to hate my brother, not realizing that in reality I hated the false self I had become in order to survive.

It would take me nearly three decades to realize that I truly had another choice: to be myself. And that being myself was not only enough, it was beautiful!

Studies have shown that the trauma of separation from love has a direct effect on the brain and on the balance of hemispheric brain functioning. A part of the brain called the hypothalamus plays a unique role in our defense against psychic pain that I believe eventually leads to the formation of the ego. This critical area of our brain plays an important function in relation to the nervous system and emotions, receiving signals of physical and emotional pain, as well as other intense emotions; it is in effect a collecting center for information concerning the well-being of the mind and body or lack thereof. Asthma, high blood pressure, hypertension, loss of appetite or overeating, insomnia or oversleeping, lack of concentration, and other common ailments are all indirectly controlled by the hypothalamus. These ailments may be psychosomatic cries for help from a young child who is frightened, lonely or feeling cut off from love.

Janov believes that childhood trauma can permanently affect the hypothalamus:

The hypothalamus is the central area where feelings
become translated into physical reality. . . . It regulates
many vital life systems . . . and as such controls the
equilibrium of the body. Thus it can be called the
body's hormonostat. Because the hormonostat is situ-
ated so delicately within the feeling circuits of the
brain, I believe that childhood trauma can alter its set
point permanently.[7]

If trauma can so drastically alter the delicate feeling circuits in the developing brain of the child, this
leads us to the conclusion that early childhood psychic
pain can severely stunt emotional growth. In that
regard, research shows that the pain and pleasure centers in the hypothalamus play a key role in this process.
For example, studies in animals have conclusively
shown that prolonged stimulation of the pain center
*can inhibit the pleasure center and eventually all memories
of pleasure,* cause peripheral psychosomatic effects, and
even *lead to death* if this stimulation is experienced over
a prolonged period of time.[8]

These facts do much to explain why we forget
our original state of soul consciousness: The psychic
pain associated with our primal separation from love
takes precedence over, and finally erases, the memory
of our original joy. Experiencing the sheer intensity of
those early primal feelings of pain and aloneness feels
like a kind of death process—which, in fact, it is.

Allow me then to restate my thesis: We instinctively seek to avoid that black hole or well of grief at
all costs, and so to defend ourselves against this threat,

we create an ego that can hold back the onslaught of repressed emotions. This is a tragic yet necessary survival gesture that all of us make without understanding the consequences. This is why I call it a "no-choice" situation.

We also pay a tremendous price for this defense against pain, a price that has profound consequences for our well-being. I hypothesize that in our original state of soul consciousness, the left and right hemispheres of the brain are in balance; the hypothalamus is processing the corresponding nerve impulses that travel through the body, and we as children experience a state of inner unity. We are not afraid to love, to trust, and to express our feelings, and happiness is our natural state. There is little, if any, fear—picture, for instance, an infant in a stroller beaming happily and unselfconsciously at total strangers. Sadly, fear and the repression of authentic feelings is something we as children learn from interacting with others who are already living in states of chronic fear. Eventually we enclose ourselves in an ego cocoon in order to survive.

When emotional healing finally begins, the emotional fears of the ego do not simply die away all at once. They are rather like the layers of an onion that eventually must be peeled away until we reach the true self at our core. With each layer that is peeled away, we experience a mixture of sadness and joy—the sadness of the original pain with which each layer was put in place and the joy that results because each layer peeled away brings us one layer closer to the core of love deepest within us. The more we are able to surrender to our deepest feelings, the closer we come to that core and the more powerful becomes the psychic pull of our state of soul consciousness residing within.

The only way to traverse the black tunnel of fear and psychic pain from which the ego is born is to fully open our hearts, stop being victims, and take full accountability for our original pain and the decisions we made from that pain.

Only then can we reach what I call the place of choice.

Only then can we finally choose love in the face of the original pain that caused us to close our hearts.

Only then can the butterfly of self-love and joy emerge from the cocoon of repression!

8

the nine stages of the Cycle of Life

We shall not cease from exploration and the end of all our exploring will be to arrive where we started and know the place for the first time.

—T.S. Eliot

The outline of the Cycle of Life that I present in this chapter describes the process—depicted in a series of nine stages—of our apparent loss and eventual recovery of our contact with the Unified Field of love. The great Cycle of Life starts in the primal state of soul consciousness, which begins in the womb, if not before. It ends with our final return to the place where we started out, having now gained the ability to know it (as T.S. Eliot would put it) for the very first time.

STAGE ONE
"I Am Joy, I Am Alone"

Our birth is but a sleep and a forgetting.

The soul that rises with us, our life's star,
hath had elsewhere its setting and cometh from afar.

Not in entire forgetfulness and not in utter
nakedness—but trailing clouds of glory do we come
from God, who is our home.

Heaven lies about us in our infancy.

—William Wordsworth

In the innocent state that begins in the womb, life
has implicit meaning and purpose within a loving plan.
The predominant feeling of Stage One is therefore
one of joy and wonder. In his compelling book *Birth
Without Violence,* the renowned French pediatrician
Frederick Leboyer describes the profundity of this
state. The newborn has just emerged from the terrifying tunnel of the birth passage, coming forth perhaps
directly from the Unified Field:

> This first look is unforgettable. Immense, deep, grave,
> intense, these eyes say: "Where am I? What has hap-
> pened to me?"

> We feel in this baby such utter concentration, such
> astonishment, such depth of curiosity, that we are
> overcome. We discover beyond any doubt, that a
> *person* is there. . . . We see—what should have been
> obvious—that far from being a beginning, birth is only
> a passage. And that this creature who is looking at us,
> questioning us, "has been" already for a long time.[1]

Leboyer was a pediatrician of the soul who changed our understanding of infant birth. For many years, most pediatricians yanked and then spanked a child out of its original blissful habitat.² But Leboyer sought to maintain, throughout the already traumatic birth process, the infant's nurturing connection to what we have called the Unified Field of love. Leboyer's compassionate birth method has inspired many pediatricians and midwives, as it far better prepares a child for its journey through life than the cold and unfeeling "yank and spank" delivery.

As you will notice in the Cycle of Life chart on page 81, I use a triangle within a circle as a symbol of the inner unity of this stage. The symbol also signifies a balance of so-called left-brain qualities (rational/analytical/creative/masculine) and right-brain qualities (feeling/intuitive/receptive/feminine). In Stage One, both brain modes are in balance and the heart is open. The child is in a state of soul consciousness.

STAGE TWO
"Who I Am Is Not Enough"

We are each a unique end product of the cosmic evolution of love, and so we are all born with an incredible capacity for joy and love. But we arrive in an utterly helpless, primal state as if we were still in the womb; we are not yet anchored in the Unified Field of love through mature clarity and discrimination. So

The Cycle of Life

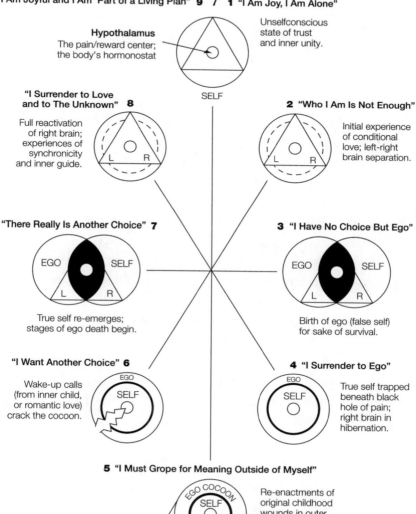

"I Am Joyful and I Am Part of a Living Plan" **9** / **1** "I Am Joy, I Am Alone"

Hypothalamus
The pain/reward center;
the body's hormonostat

Unselfconscious
state of trust
and inner unity.

SELF

**"I Surrender to Love
and to The Unknown" 8**

Full reactivation
of right brain;
experiences of
synchronicity
and inner guide.

2 "Who I Am Is Not Enough"

Initial experience
of conditional
love; left-right
brain separation.

"There Really Is Another Choice" 7

EGO   SELF

True self re-emerges;
stages of ego death begin.

3 "I Have No Choice But Ego"

EGO   SELF

Birth of ego (false self)
for sake of survival.

"I Want Another Choice" 6

EGO
SELF

Wake-up calls
(from inner child,
or romantic love)
crack the cocoon.

4 "I Surrender to Ego"

EGO
SELF

True self trapped
beneath black
hole of pain;
right brain in
hibernation.

5 "I Must Grope for Meaning Outside of Myself"

EGO COCOON
SELF

Re-enactments of
original childhood
wounds in outer
relationships.

it doesn't take long, or much, for each of us to be frightened, badgered, intimidated, and confused out of our original state of soul consciousness and forced into the realm of ego consciousness.

Very quickly we begin to see and feel that people close to us are afraid to love deeply, afraid to trust, afraid to express their truest feelings, afraid to be happy, afraid to be who they are. In fact, the adults around us expect, even demand, that we become like them—an untrue and inauthentic self.

The method adults unwittingly use to teach us this new and unnatural way of being is *conditional love*. When as very young children we are loved with conditions and reservations, adults are planting the first seeds of self-doubt. The message coming across to us is *Who you are is not enough*. And this message is continually being reinforced by the simple fact that we are highly vulnerable to the fear of losing the love of our primary caregivers. We experience an implied threat: *Fulfill my expectations, become who I think you should be, or risk losing my love*. By submitting to the implicit demands of conditional love, we lose our natural state of soul consciousness, and with it, the ability to be our authentic and natural self.

STAGE THREE
"I Have No Choice But Ego!"

Most of us as young children are treated as objects and are manipulated into being something other than who we are. Our deepest feelings are consistently ignored or misunderstood, and as a result, our original unity of self gets fragmented. Increasingly, we feel painfully isolated and confused, at times to the point of despair.

In Stage Three, we are torn between two diametrically opposed realms: Our naturally blissful state of soul consciousness stands on one side, against the unnatural, awkward, and painful ego world of adults on the other. We are already under duress from the adults around us; and now we must placate them by somehow fashioning a new identity through trial and error, in order to earn their conditional love and acceptance.

Stage Three is one of tragic struggle and misunderstanding. When we attempt to express the pain and confusion of this transitional process, no one really understands us. What adult can comprehend the profound existential crisis endured by every infant forced to relinquish the bliss of soul consciousness in ex-change for the bewildering and disturbing state of ego consciousness? And what infant is able to articulate this crisis? What young child can find a way to express to others that no one truly sees him or her?

As infants and young children, we are seemingly helpless in a world of superior powers and desperately in need of an unconditional love that is not available;

at some point, entering into ego consciousness appears to us to be our sole means of survival. In fact, *the birth of the ego is a kind of death-for-the-sake-of-survival.*

Stage Three is about protecting ourselves from feelings of profound anguish. Because we as young children cannot bear this anguish for very long, we are finally driven to separate from the primal state of inner unity and soul consciousness. And there is no choice! Gradually, we learn to mistrust our deepest feelings. Slowly but surely we are forced to undergo a traumatic psychic birth into the egoic "reality" of our parents and culture. And this transition is so bewildering that our true self retreats into an inner cell. The self now dwells in a prison of aloneness, a cocoon of safety.[3]

The pain of not being loved for who we are is of such deep psychic proportions that death or madness might occur if we did not instinctively armor ourselves against it. Ego consciousness (defined as repression of and defense against feelings, manipulation of others and the environment; acting out as self-protection, and so on) is the only logical survival response. In other words, disconnecting from the Field becomes a chronic survival strategy in Stage Three.

STAGE FOUR
"I Surrender to Ego"

In this stage there is even more tragedy. As we have seen, the authentic or whole self includes the feeling/intuitive/receptive right brain with its inherent connection to soul consciousness. And in response to intense psychic pain, the right brain in Stage Four goes into hibernation within the ego's protective cocoon, and hypothalamic reactions are triggered that literally halt our emotional growth. As we grow older, *we leave behind an inner child whose development has been arrested.* This inner child, who we will encounter in Session One to come, has gone into hiding within the ego cocoon. This trapped child remains there, avoiding its pain, and waiting to somehow be seen and unconditionally loved.

As a therapist, there is no doubt in my mind that a scared and emotionally trapped inner child resides within each of my clients. I invariably find that this inner child is convinced that being himself or herself is not enough, that he or she is bad, unworthy of love, and perhaps even evil.

In Stage Four our true self is buried beneath an inner black hole of pain. We have lost all sense of having a place within a loving plan, and for too many of us, we have lost all sense that life has meaning or purpose. We naturally resort to the fearful strategies of the ego; we learn to grope for meaning outside ourselves and disregard the cues coming from within.

The black circle on the Cycle of Life chart around the self represents this black hole that now operates beneath the surface of our awareness, overshadowing our consciousness and limiting our freedom of being.

STAGE FIVE
"I Must Grope for Meaning Outside Myself"

A person in a state of solidified ego consciousness exerts every effort, without awareness, to avoid the black hole of pain. At this stage we are reluctant to feel, explore, or express these deeply repressed feelings. *In fact, we have created the ego precisely to avoid them.*[4] At the same time, we are desperately looking outside ourselves for love, the deepest feeling of all.

In Stage Five we come face-to-face with the core problem in the Cycle of Life: On the one hand, the love we truly seek can only be found within. On the other hand, *this is precisely the place we dare not look* and that we chronically avoid! This is the great paradox of our human predicament.

In other words, in order to find that love we so desperately need, we must do the last thing in the world we wish to do—the very thing that we painstakingly built an ego to shield ourselves against: Rather than look outside ourselves for love, we must instead face and feel through the inner black hole of pain that separates us from our conscious connection to the Unified Field. Until we are able to face these feelings, we tend to become what we fear we really are deep down: fat, ugly, dumb, stupid, damaged, bad—in essence, unlovable or unworthy of love. Our romantic attachments are therefore bound to fail.

But even in our Stage Five state of separated ego consciousness, we are continually being driven from within to break free of the ego's cocoon. Something hidden within us knows we must find and surrender to our deepest pain in order to reconnect to the joy that lies beneath it. When we are in Stage Five, the key way we act on this urge is to re-enact our original child-hood struggle in our relationships. We do this by liter-ally creating an adult experience of the way we were most deeply wounded as children.

This re-enactment usually occurs in our romantic relationships. For example, we become attracted to men or women who seemingly end up wounding us in just the way our mothers or fathers did. I find this pat-tern continually repeated in the lives of my patients, and for some time I found it occurring in my own life. For many years I was attracted to women like my mother—beautiful, cold, and emotionally unavail-able—even preferring them to warm, loving women. As such, I repeatedly re-created my original wounding relationship with my mother until I resolved it by going within and finally embracing my wounded self. In the same way, we may re-create familiar negative sibling dynamics, abusive sexual dynamics, and other formative childhood relationship traumas.

We all tend to repeat certain unhealthy patterns. Our culture usually views such patterns in purely negative terms as merely self-destructive behavior. But I believe there is a deeper truth here: Our hidden self, the wounded child within, *guides* us into these relationships for a reason. I believe that these so-called re-enactments are unconscious attempts to fully experience and finally resolve the original wounding separations from love, joy, and soul consciousness that occurred in our earliest years. But until we realize this, we tend to merely repeat, rather than resolve, these negative patterns. The re-enactments remain grade D movies with no redeeming value, always leading us to the original pain, which we again repress, only to repeat the re-enactment in a future relationship.

In one of my favorite early sessions with my clients, Session Two, we review all their important love relationships in their Life Chart. The purpose is to help my clients see how they have manifested these relationships as a means of working out unresolved issues that existed in their primary childhood relationships, usually with their parents. What's interesting is that their current or most recent relationship tends to be with someone who is very much like themselves. As a result, they cannot easily avoid their unresolved fears and pain, because their partner is a mirror for them.

Once they see these repeating patterns clearly, they can now begin taking full accountability for the decisions they made because of—or to avoid—their black hole of pain. At last! They can allow themselves to see their life as a meaningful quest to be fully embraced rather than a painful struggle to be avoided. They then begin to glimpse the rich possibility of a life lived in the context of a loving plan rather than a life embedded in the suffocating world of ego consciousness. This realization is the beginning of their return to a state of soul consciousness.

STAGE SIX
"I Want Another Choice"

A dream is nothing but a message that comes to us from the dark, all-unifying world of the psyche. What would be more natural, when we have lost ourselves amid the endless particulars and isolated details of the world's surface, than to knock on the door of dreams and inquire of them the bearings which could bring us closer to the basic facts of human existence.

—Carl Jung

Love is the ultimate wake-up call—for it has the power to present us with another choice! In this phase a love relationship comes along that cracks open the ego cocoon, or perhaps the inner child issues a wake-up call through some other vehicle. It is only in Stage Six that we begin to glimpse another world, a deeper inner world that calls to us through dreams, synchronistic events, and soul-based intuition.

The full experience and expression of our deepest feelings within a supportive and accepting environment is the optimal path to a more balanced state of inner unity. Love, the ultimate feeling, is now calling us from our deepest core to enter this path. It is inviting us to surrender through and beyond our fears, resistance, and pain. And the ego is beginning now to yield to love because *it intuitively recognizes love as the "medicine" it was always seeking.*

The worst prison is a closed heart! Our journey to inner freedom and unity doesn't really take off until we open our hearts. Opening the heart and yielding to love is the most important step on the path that leads us back to soul consciousness. When this happens, the authentic child within and the feeling/intuitive/receptive right brain, with its connection to the Unified Field, are now awakened from their long hibernation within the ego's cocoon. We can begin the process of being truly inner-directed.

It is a joyful and grand event when we realize that our ultimate guidance comes from within, not from "out there." When this happens, we have begun to re-establish a connection to the state of soul consciousness that we lost in childhood by trying to become what others wanted us to be in order to gain their love and approval. Only when we are fully inner-directed are we ready to allow and endure the death of the ego and the birth of our true self.

The more we hear and respond to this call from within, the more clearly we see that our only true choice is to listen and follow. At Stage Six it becomes too painful to resist.

STAGE SEVEN
"There Really Is Another Choice"

There comes a time for the rosebud when it becomes more painful to remain tight in the bud than to blossom.

—Anais Nin

In Stage Seven, the butterfly of who you really are is emerging from its cocoon!

At this point, we become aware that the ego is an obstacle to our freedom and happiness. We no longer need it for protection and survival in the way we previously did. Yet we can "shed" it only to the degree that we trust our inner guidance. We can let it go only to the extent that we are strong enough to face and feel through our deepest feelings, fears, and pain to the spring of love and joy at our core.

At this point of convergence with our true self, the primal state of soul consciousness becomes an incredibly attractive force. The spiritual gravity of the Unified Field draws us from within, much like the "omega" that Teilhard de Chardin has written about. The more we trust and surrender to this inner process and our deepest feelings, the more powerful and urgent this pull becomes. There is now another choice, and we no longer choose to resist.

Our consideration of Stage Seven brings us to the subject of *ego death,* or final ego transcendence, that is spoken of in all the mystical and wisdom traditions. The phases of ego death listed below follow Elisabeth

Kubler-Ross's five phases of the process of physical death—but with one additional phase. I've attached my own specialized meaning to each phase. They are as follows:

1. Denial—Everything is fine, there is nothing missing in my life.

2. Anger—I can't stay in control and manipulate things anymore; it's not working and it's making me mad.

3. Bargaining—I'll cling to anything to avoid losing control, facing the unknown, and going through the well of grief deep inside me.

4. Depression—Why am I feeling so sad? Why does it seem to go so deep, and why can't I get out of this grief?

5. Acceptance—I'm feeling sad and there's nothing I can do about it. I can't deny or resist these deep feelings any longer. I know they've been there a long time. I'll just let them be what they are.

6. Surrender—What is this joy and excitement I'm feeling beneath this deep sadness? It doesn't have anything to do with someone else. It's me! I'm finally beginning to trust my deepest feelings, and I'm feeling a growing sense that everything is going to be all right.

Remember, there is only one way through the black tunnel of original pain, aloneness, and despair from which the ego and ego consciousness are born. And that is to stop denying love and, next, to take full accountability or responsibility for our original pain and the decisions we made from that pain.

Only then can the butterfly that is the Stage Seven self emerge from its cocoon!

STAGE EIGHT
"I Surrender to Love and to the Unknown"

To relinquish ego is to relinquish all desire to gain power over others. Now energy that was previously used for ego defense becomes available for creative use in fulfilling one's function within a loving plan. The feeling/intuitive/receptive right brain awakens into balance. We look forward to the unknown, for we now intuitively sense that within the mystery of the unknown is a loving plan at work; and the more we trust the unknown, the more deeply we allow ourselves to feel—the less we need the ego for protection and survival.

Remember, it was our fears that our ego was protecting us from and that brought the ego into being in the first place. But once we are no longer afraid to feel to our depths, the ego's problematic, aggressive/defensive functioning can now give way to the simple and free functioning of our soul-conscious self.

In Stage Eight, we are now able to surrender to this authentic, feeling self and experience our true beauty. Now the unconscious, separative strategies and devices of the ego are increasingly shed like an old skin. The mind is surrendering to the guidance of the soul. And what lies ahead of us is our final yielding to, and taking responsibility for, our own joyous function within the loving plan.

Paul Williams describes this stage in *Das Energi:*

> Sooner or later a person begins to realize that everything that happens to him is perfect, relates directly to who he is, had to happen, was meant to happen, and plays its role in fulfilling his destiny. When he encounters difficulty, he no longer complains. Instead, he asks himself, What can I learn from this? How will it strengthen me, make me more aware?
>
> Strengthened by this simple notion, simple awareness that life is perfect, that all things come at the proper moment, and that he is always the perfect person for the situation he finds himself in, a person begins to feel more and more in tune with his inner nature and begins to find it easier and easier to do what he knows is right.
>
> The affirmation of one's own life, the acceptance of one's destiny as it manifests itself in each moment, is the supreme act of faith.
>
> It's a hell of a commitment![5]

STAGE NINE
"I Am Joyful and I Am Part of a Loving Plan"

The Cycle of Life completes itself when we fully surrender to our original connection to the Unified Field, return to a state of soul consciousness, and take full responsibility for our own unique function within an evolving loving plan.

We are once again in a fully loving and trusting state of wholeness, and this inner well-being is being transmitted to the body's vegetative functions via the hypothalamus. (Some of my clients are literally rejuvenated by ten years when they transition from lives controlled by fear to lives controlled by love.) In Stage Nine our life has new meaning and purpose and we are no longer controlled by fear.

We now begin to see all around us (even beneath the violence and inhumanity that permeate our world) a slowly unfolding loving plan, and our part in it becomes fully evident. I like to refer to *Christ consciousness* as an equivalent to soul consciousness, because I see the love Jesus manifested in his life as the same love that is deepest within us all. But the compassion of the Buddha, the Virgin Mary, or any other divinely inspired spiritual figure who resonates with our innate state of soul consciousness can also be an equally valid model.

Once we make a firm commitment to find and be guided by our true self and to reconnect to the Unified Field, we are on a path that will lead us through every fear and barrier that stands in the way of our living as our true self.

I often call this final process of surrender the *fires of attrition*. It is here that any remaining feelings of unworthiness and resentment are flushed out to be burned or ground away by virtue of our conscious experience of them, quite often with tears of joy. These formerly painful feelings are then replaced by feelings of worthiness and gratitude as we begin to realize how deeply we are loved—and have always been loved.

It is said that God reveals Himself only to a grateful heart. And from this place of worthiness and gratitude we are naturally drawn into service in the evolving loving plan. Being in service means taking full responsibility for what we know and expressing it in life with enthusiasm, joy, conviction, and purpose. It also means being and expressing our authentic self, regardless of the risks.

The last stage, which never ends, is fully owning and expressing the joy of who we really are. And we do this unconditionally—whether or not the people around us and closest to us are doing so.

This stage has now brought us face to face in a final confrontation with our deepest aloneness. And because we have surrendered and gone through this aloneness, we now realize that standing alone (as our authentic self, with our heart wide open) is really belonging. This level of surrender opens us up to our fullest connection to the Unified Field of love and lets

us see that we are exactly where we belong in this loving plan. We now have the courage to own our joy in
a world of victims!

Carlos Castaneda sums it up well:

> Only the love for this splendorous being can give free-
> dom to a warrior's spirit. And freedom is joy, efficien-
> cy, and abandon in the face of any odds.

> That is the last lesson. It is always left for the very last
> moment—for the moment of ultimate solitude when
> a man faces his death and aloneness. Only then does it
> make sense. The twilight is the crack between the
> worlds. It is the door to the unknown.[6]

9

introduction
to the
session
work

The next seven chapters are designed to lead you through the substance and detail of my work in the same way that I lead my clients in actual sessions. The work is action-oriented, powerful, and deep, and it is directed at producing results. It is designed to guide clients through ingrained patterns of self-sabotage, fear, doubt, and emotional pain into what I call a "place of choice"—a new experience of personal freedom and soul consciousness. This work is not for the faint of heart. It takes great courage and commitment. I do not put Band-Aids on egos!

Most people who come to me are looking for love in relationship but, sadly, have not claimed it within themselves. Some of my clients come long distances and want to go through the sessions in the shortest possible time (such as five to six days). Many are themselves therapists. Most have tried different methods for overcoming patterns of self-sabotage and are excited as well as fearful about experiencing my intensive short-term self-healing work.

In doing this work, I suggest that you read no more than one session chapter per day. Consider this material deeply in your heart and make a commitment to actively engage in the assigned homework before going on to the next chapter. Unless you do this, effective progress may not occur, because each session and its homework provides the foundation for you to engage the next session. Above all, *don't go faster than you can process the information and authentically fulfill the homework assignment.* You may also find that you need more than one day to do any particular session. So take that time and don't skip steps. The important thing is to do the homework thoroughly. There is no change without action, and only action changes knowledge into wisdom. *So do the work, and don't just think about it!*

When you go through the seven sessions, it's as though there are two people listening: your ego personality and the child within. Your inner child is your original soul-conscious self who wants to be acknowledged and loved at last for who he or she is. This work is about finding and healing that child within and rediscovering your original, joyful self.

Also, pay attention to your dreams. They are often messages from the soul that are meant to be enlisted in the conscious unraveling of your ego. Keep a dream journal near your bed and interpret your dreams in relation to whatever issues, feelings, and memories you are presently experiencing.

You are initiating a profound process by doing this work, and many feelings, emotions, memories, and fears may rise to the surface. You don't need to control them, change them, or get rid of them. You simply need to feel them in a state of openness and trust. At times you may feel that you've opened up Pandora's box. This is good, for all the undigested emotion and experience you've stored away can now become the treasure that reveals important details and meanings of your life's quest. Always remember, beneath your deepest pain is your deeper joy, intention, and purpose! The path to the soul is through doors of fear and pain. And you must learn not to be controlled by fear if you hope to reach the holy grail of who you really are.

Between these sessions I will share stories, my own and others, to demonstrate how these processes can unfold in real lives. So try to experience me as a coach who has done this work (not as a therapist listening from an emotional distance and telling you what to do). I will help create an environment in which the lost child within you feels safe to come out and express itself and in which the adult in you feels safe and clear enough to go through these processes.

I formalize this venture into very sacred inner space by having my clients put on Chinese slippers when they come into my office for each session.

Wherever you are, consider doing something similar as you begin each session. By formally or ritually entering a sacred space within yourself, you affirm and focus your purpose and intention. So find a way to enter that sacred space, whether it is through prayer, chanting, meditation, lighting a candle or incense, ringing a bell, listening to a song that has great meaning for you— whatever works for you. You can also decorate or arrange your external environment in any way that helps you to enter this sacred space.

In the first session you will be working with childhood pictures and memories. Below is a picture drawn by a six-year-old, Samantha, who was having a very difficult time in school as she struggled with a traumatic situation at home.

Her picture characterizes what many of my clients are feeling when they come to see me. She has drawn a headstone, which she tells me belongs to her buried heart. As you can see, her hand is reaching up from below the surface of the grave. From beneath her fear, she is reaching out for help. Perhaps you are, too. Samantha wants to be seen. She wants someone to take her hand and walk with her through her fears. She wants permission to open her heart. In my one session with Samantha, I took her hand in mine and she opened her heart because she knew I was seeing her. (Children are closer than adults to a place of trust and to their original state of soul consciousness because they have not spent years armoring themselves against love and their deepest feelings.)

As such, I am now taking your hand in mine and telling you that you can now face any feelings you may be afraid of. The stories I share will help you trust this process and, like Samantha, feel supported.

You are strong enough to do this work, and go through your deepest fears. You are capable of going through the well of grief you have carried with you all these years to the source of joy that lives at your core. All I can do is lead you to that place of choice. And if you choose, you can now open your heart, surrender to love, heal yourself, take your part in the universal loving plan—and give the world the gift of yourself.

Homework:

In preparation for our journey, gather some pictures of yourself as a very young child particularly from birth to age ten. *Buy a blank journal for writing down your notes, and treat it is if it were a sacred text.* Begin now to assemble and write down as much information as you can find about your birth and the family circumstances surrounding it.

– Were you wanted?

– Did your parents want a boy or girl?

– Was it a normal birth?

– Were you separated from your mother after birth, and if so, for how long?

– Were any other siblings born after you, and if so, when?

– How did you react to each younger sibling's birth?

– In early childhood what traumatic events—physical injuries, painful separations, wounding emotional encounters— deeply affected you?

The first session will help you fully focus on these questions, and the childhood pictures will help you make emotional connections. One of my favorite childhood pictures is this picture of myself at three years old. As you can see, I am literally radiating with joy. This picture, which is now hanging on my office wall, has been an important reminder for me that beneath my well of grief was a spring of heartfelt joy. If you can find such a joyful childhood photo of yourself, put it where you can view it often. It will serve as an important reminder of the joyful child who still lives within you, waiting to be discovered.

So, shall we begin?

10

finding the child within yourself

session one

We all shut down emotionally as children, usually between birth and the age of seven. This work focuses on the joyful child you once were who still lives inside you. When the psychic pain of your original separation from love drove this child into hiding, *your whole life became a quest* to rediscover your true self, to open your heart again and return to your original state of soul consciousness. Shutting down emotionally can occur for any number of reasons, including a difficult or traumatic birth; the sudden addition of siblings who reduced the amount of attention you received; parental conflicts, separations, or divorces; the death of a parent or other close family member; and severe physical or emotional traumas that have resulted from accidental injuries, illness, and physical or sexual abuse. Even prenatal events can set up lifelong painful emotional or psychological patterns.

You may well have experienced traumatic events that affected you while you were in your mother's womb. (One of my clients, a young woman whose mother attempted to abort her six months in utero, was almost stillborn. She had lived in a kind of prolonged panic until she did this work.)

So now, get out your sacred journal and answer the following questions in writing:

— How much have you found out about the circumstances surrounding your conception, your wombtime, and your birth?

— Were you a wanted child?

— Were you an accidental child?

— Was your mother abused, ill, or depressed while she was pregnant with you?

— What happened when you were born?

— What happened after you were born?

— Having found out as much as you can about these circumstances, examine the pictures of yourself as a child.

— Can you see the point where you emotionally checked out?

— Can you find the earliest picture that shows a change, a diminishing of the joy of infancy that may be visible in earlier pictures?

— Do you recall any incidents that may explain this change of appearance? Even if you don't have any pictures of yourself as a child, a part of you already knows where or when that change occurred. Think back, feel back, to that time.

— What decisive event or events occurred that were more than you were able to handle emotionally?

— How old were you at the time?

— How did you feel?

— How did you change as a response?

Write your answers in your sacred journal.

Consider all you know about your birth and very early years in order to best determine where you closed your heart, and where the feeling "Being me is not enough" drove you inside and away from love. Perhaps what you felt was "There must be something wrong with me" or "I'm a bad girl" or "I'm no good" or "Nobody likes me."

— How emotionally available was your mother?

— How emotionally available was your father?

— Examine all other key relationships you had as a child—with siblings, grandparents, friends.

— What feelings can you recall? Look for feelings of sadness, anger, despair, fear, aloneness, bewilderment.

— What conditions did you experience at that time?

— What meanings did you make out of your experience?

— Did you decide that you were bad, not loved, not special, unimportant, not lovable?

— Did you decide that certain people were mean or scary or unpredictable or undependable?

— How did you decide to act as a result?

— Did you decide to hide, to not be seen, to try harder to get attention, to protect yourself, to close your heart?

— Did you decide not to like others, not to trust others, not to let any one get close to you?

— Do you remember when this happened and why and how it felt and how you were after that?

It's amazing what we can recall when we go back to look in this way.

If you really engage this process with great focus and intention, you will begin to recall events that coincide with the visible changes you see in your photos or with your memories of the changes that occurred in yourself. Make notes of all these recollections. They will be useful later. Through this process of internal questioning and recollection, you will see how you made decisions and then acted on what you felt were your only possible choices.

At this point, let's briefly review the early stages of the Cycle of Life: We saw that when traumatic events occur in early childhood, we feel lost and wounded. We then set out to redefine ourselves and prove our worth so that we can feel accepted. Usually we take on the behaviors, attitudes, and values of someone else— someone bigger, better, stronger. From a place of aloneness, we may watch those close to us to learn new ways to act, or act out, new ways to learn anything that will help us receive more attention and love. *We become, by trial and error, whatever we believe we have to become in order to be loved.* It is out of this strategy that the ego is born. A whole new personality is created from choices and decisions we make to avoid pain and get love!

When I was taken away from my grandfather and our maid, Delia, the being I was literally went into hibernation. A new "I"—one locked in a state of ego consciousness—emerged as a willful and self-protective response to the pain I could not bear to feel. I was convinced that I had no one, except my twin, who truly cared for me. Closing my heart and shutting down my emotions was my way of choosing to survive.

We've all lived some version of this archetypal story. And this "choice" that each of us made was neither right nor wrong, neither good nor bad. It is nothing to regret; it was inevitable. It's what all children *do* to adapt and survive in a world dominated by ego consciousness, a world where most children are seemingly manipulated and controlled through conditional approval and conditional love—not to mention punishment of various kinds that appear, *to a child*, to be the tangible cessation of love.

Remember, at this vulnerable point in your development, *you had no choice!* And this no-choice decision you made is what allowed you to survive and to get to where you are right now. Now, perhaps you are ready to make a different choice. I suggest that this is the perfect time. It's your turn!

Let's briefly consider the story and pictures of a former client. This is Maxine, a lovely little girl born to

parents who really wanted a boy. They even called her Max for the first 18 years of her life. In a picture taken shortly after her birth, you can clearly see that she is radiating joy in a natural state of love and soul consciousness. I have also seen another photo (not shown) of Maxine at just a few months old that seems to reflect confusion, perhaps because of her parents' disappointment that she is not a boy.

In the next photo, Maxine, now a year old, is using

anger to cover up the sadness that was visible in the preceding photos. This little girl has already closed her heart and emotionally checked out, and her eyes reflect the sadness of this inescapable choice.

 When you examine your own pictures, you will also be able to see where you emotionally checked out; you may begin to see the point where you became something other than yourself. The openness and purity evident in many infant photos is gradually replaced by a mask whose purpose is to deflect pain and to please others in order to earn love. This mask — the face of the ego—often reflects a sense of confusion, anxiety, and fear. It is a plea for acceptance and love.

In Maxine's pictures we can see this transition from the original soul-conscious self to painful ego consciousness. Remember, for the first 18 years of her life Maxine's parents called her Max, a name for the son they really wanted—and a daily reminder to Maxine that who she was, was not enough. As you might imagine, it didn't take long for this message to sink in and have its devastating effect on her life and relationships. Once again, the lesson is that *we all want to be seen and loved for the person we really are.* And when we are not, the psychic pain soon becomes more than we can bear.

The purpose of this photo exercise is for you to

literally see and connect again to that lost child within you who still wants to be seen and loved for who he or she really is. You are the only one now who can heal this child. And you can only do this by reaching inside and embracing this child. If painful feelings arise, just feel them, breathe deeply into them, and let the tears flow if they come. As you exhale, spontaneously allow any sounds to groan out of you. Allow yourself to fully feel any pain that is still there.

But it's important that you not focus on being a victim. There is a difference between genuine sorrow and self-pity. Being a victim is how the ego defends itself against feeling a deeper pain. So instead of focusing on the story about how you were wounded, focus on the feelings themselves. You can only heal the wound by surrendering through the well of grief and this child's pain without being a victim and without denying love. *Remember, most of the people we felt the deepest pain with were people we also deeply loved or wanted to love!* Take total accountability for your pain by not blaming anyone for it and by not denying love! This is the decisive step (which we will cover in an upcoming session) toward full release and surrender to the little child within you who wants to love so deeply.

As you deep-breathe into the pain, completely let go and simply feel it. Don't try and get rid of it, change it, or make it go away. Feel all the way through it. Completely surrender to these feelings and express them with your breath, with sounds. The more you are able to feel and release them, and the further you pass through the inner black tunnel of pain, the closer you will be to touching the place of your original joy. Don't be afraid to take a time-out during this inner process if you feel the need for one.

Please consider this concept as you do this exercise: We all wanted to be on this planet, regardless of the current circumstances of our lives. I know I did! I remember my mother once revealing to me with a deep sense of guilt (long after I found my true self) that I was conceived in anger. And I immediately replied: "But I wanted to be here! I wouldn't have missed this for anything! So you're off the hook!" In that spontaneous moment of self-revelation and celebration I not only took accountability for myself but I also helped my mother move beyond her feelings of guilt.

You can do this too. It is now your turn to own your right to be you and to celebrate yourself!

If you need support right now in affirming this, write these words down and keep them handy: "It's my turn!" This means it is your turn to fully acknowledge and accept yourself for who you are. It is your turn to finally give yourself a voice and a choice. And you will do this by finding and healing the child within yourself who shut down when the pain of not being loved for who he or she was became too much to bear. Perhaps you have always thought that other people's needs were more important than yours. But right now it's time to be "selfish" and take your turn, because the lost child within you has always longed for you to do just this.

Now once again, find the most joyful photograph of yourself as a child and keep it close to you as you do this work. It is this child who has led you to this book and into every significant relationship in your life, seeking to be recognized, heard, and loved. This is what this work is all about: finding the child within you, giving that child a voice.

Your whole intention in this session is to find the child within you, to embrace that child with total empathy and compassion, and to give that child the unconditional love he or she still needs in order to be healed. Remember, love is the ultimate healing force and the deepest feeling within us all. To find this depth of love, you must be willing to feel through all the feelings that stand between you and this love, which is our original state of soul consciousness.

When you fully engage this process, you may spontaneously recall events in early childhood in which you made life-altering decisions to become someone other than your true self in order to avoid feeling pain, to please others, and to earn their love. Within a very short period after experiencing these painful recollections, joy may begin bubbling up in you and through you! You may recall joyful events that have been buried beneath the deep pain you have been carrying for most of your life. Or you may simply feel the ecstatic energy that is triggered when these painful ego patterns are seen, understood, and released. It is as if the psychic energy long trapped in these ego patterns is now suddenly set free and is flooding through you.

When you reach this place in your inner journey, everything is accelerated. Until now you've mostly traveled on the Ego Local, which is fueled by fear and unworthiness. But now you are boarding the Heart Express. It is fueled by love and compassion, which begins with your relationship to yourself and to the child within. On the Heart Express you learn to transcend yourself by truly being yourself and eventually by empowering others in their own process. At that point, your life becomes filled with joy, intention, and purpose, with a deep awareness that your life is being divinely guided and that you have a part to play in this loving plan.

But the journey does not really begin until you fully open your heart!

We are all emissaries of love on a mission to a planet that is in the process of being born. The most important birth in our life occurs when we open our heart and deliver the child in ourselves from a place of fear and aloneness to a place of trust and love. The young lady whose mother tried to abort her, and many other of my clients, have done this and are now living their original joy and giving the gift of themselves to the world. This can happen to you as well.

Homework:

On page 119 you will find a blank Life Chart. Using the abbreviated Cycle of Life chart presented in Chapter 8 on page 82, complete your own Life Chart by listing, in timeline fashion, the key relationships and events that affected your life. Place the events on the Joy or Despair side of the chart centerline—a kind of positive/negative emotional Richter scale. You will notice that the places where you checked out are places of despair.

While you're doing this, spend time looking at your pictures. It may also be useful to reread the Life Cycle chapter to get a deeper sense of the stages we all pass through. This will help you to find those places in the details of your own life. Memories will come up. Write them down in your sacred journal. List all the important relationships in your life in which you know you were looking for love.

We will review the events and relationships of your life in the next chapter. You will be referring to your completed chart often throughout these sessions. This chart will be the working model for your journey to a place of choice. Remember to keep the childhood picture of a joyful you close by as a reminder that this is where you came from and that this is where you are heading.

Tim's Story

"Someone Is Going to Take Your Hand"

Because of my own surrender to soul consciousness and the Unified Field, I am able to enter a deep communing relationship with my clients from the very first session, and healing miracles such as Tim's story can and do happen. Let me share with you the exciting story of when I first realized this.

Tim came to see me in 1989. He was a very talented filmmaker but had never taken full responsibility for his gift because of deep issues of shame-based guilt. When, in our first session, I took him by the hand and told him that it was "his turn," he seemed deeply touched. But it was not until the next day that I learned how deep our connection was.

Although he was preparing to leave for Korea within a few days to do a major shoot, he called me the day after that session and told me, with a great deal of excitement, that he had to see me immediately.

When we got together later that day, he told me about an incident that had happened when his father was dying several years before. It seems that his father had literally died several times and then returned to a lucid conciousness before he relapsed

cont. on page 120

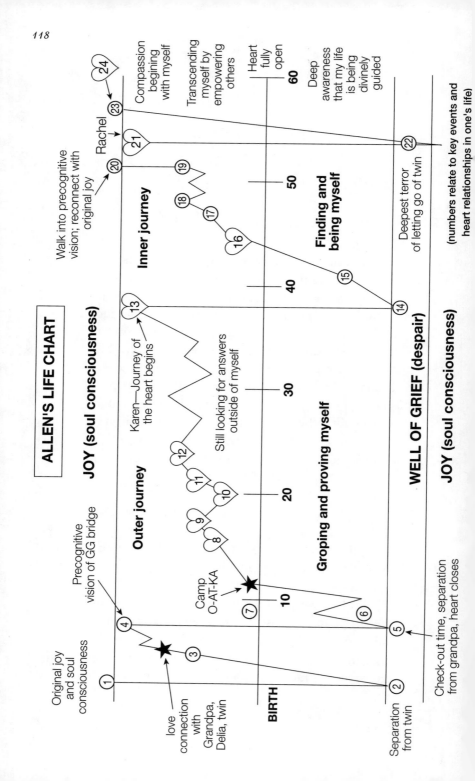

ALLEN'S LIFE CHART

JOY (soul consciousness)

WELL OF GRIEF (despair)

JOY (soul consciousness)

BIRTH

Outer journey

Groping and proving myself

Inner journey

Finding and being myself

Original joy and soul consciousness

Precognitive vision of GG bridge

love connection with Grandpa, Delia, twin

Camp O-AT-KA

Karen—Journey of the heart begins

Still looking for answers outside of myself

Walk into precognitive vision; reconnect with original joy

Rachel

Compassion begining with myself

Transcending myself by empowering others

Heart fully open

Deep awareness that my life is being divinely guided

Separation from twin

Check-out time, separation from grandpa, heart closes

Deepest terror of letting go of twin

(numbers relate to key events and heart relationships in one's life)

10 20 30 40 50 60

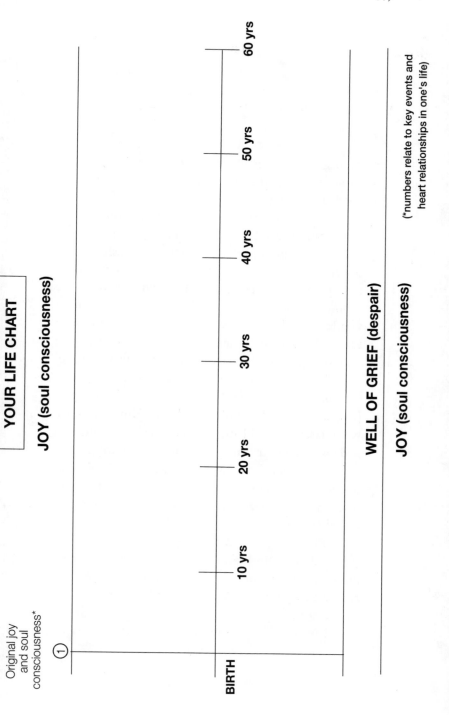

YOUR LIFE CHART

Original joy and soul consciousness*

① BIRTH

JOY (soul consciousness)

10 yrs 20 yrs 30 yrs 40 yrs 50 yrs 60 yrs

WELL OF GRIEF (despair)

JOY (soul consciousness)

(*numbers relate to key events and heart relationships in one's life)

again into a coma. During one of those lucid periods, Tim asked him, "What's it like on the other side, Dad?" His dad smiled at him and said, "Someone is going to take your hand."

Tim told me that when I had taken his hand during our first session, he had been deeply moved. Later that day, he realized that it was my hand that his dad had seen.

At that point, I got goose bumps and realized that I was indeed in a state of soul consciousness with my clients and that this state obviously existed beyond time and space. Of course, Tim's dad would have been in a state of soul consciousness when he momentarily slipped away—and in that moment he would have had access to anyone who would be loving his son unconditionally, because that loving state of consciousness exists beyond time and space.

That realization was all Tim needed to fully surrender to and trust his path through his deepest fears and guilt. He called me from Korea about a week later and told me he had cried all night and had connected his pain to the little boy within himself. He also shared how he had awakened the next day with a feeling of great exhilaration and a deep sense of inner peace, which he had never experienced before.

Tim was now on the Express!

I define the Express as a state of total surrender and trust in this process of inner unfolding. In reality, this process is a joyful child within pushing all the pain and self-doubt to the surface so that it can claim its original joy, intention, and purpose.

When Tim returned, he quickly got to the origins of his deep guilt with his mother and the moment he had shut down his feelings and decided to never let anyone in. When he reached that painful moment—which he fully surrendered to—I had him look into my eyes. I told him that his mother forgave him and that he needed to forgive himself and stop denying his gift and deep joy.

Feeling his mother's presence in the room, he tearfully forgave himself.

Remember, there are no accidents when you are on the inner path to joy and freedom. Tim found that out when he left my office that day.

As he drove away, he turned on the radio—and immediately burst into tears. "Baby Mine," a song from an early Disney movie, was playing. It was a song his mother used to sing to him as a young child. He drove to a nearby park and cried for two hours. But these were tears of joy, for now he knew that his mother had truly forgiven him and that a heavy burden of guilt and shame had been lifted from his soul.

Tim is now taking full responsibility for his life by saying yes to himself instead of no, and his life is a reflection of his inner joy, intention, and purpose.

Tim is also a good example of how virtually all the people we deeply love are affected when we make a dramatic shift in consciousness. Nearly all of Tim's brothers and sisters took a step toward inner freedom and peace of mind within six months after his shift from ego to soul consciousness.

11

understanding your life as a quest with a Life Chart

session two

Having discovered where you shut down emotionally as a child, the next step is to help you see your entire life as an inspired quest—as opposed to a grim struggle for survival.

To help you fully internalize this quest, we will work on developing new insights about your past and current relationships; we will also cultivate compassion for your choices in life so far. Doing this work will require a thorough review of your Life Chart; significant journaling in response to my questions about your chart; and the courage to openly share your quest with significant others.

But first, before we go over your chart, write once again, at the top of the page in your sacred journal, *"It's My Turn!"* Write it big and bold.

In this session, you will learn how every single relationship you have had has been a gift, and an important step in your courageous and lifelong quest to find yourself—regardless of any pain or despair you may have experienced in that relationship.

Your task in Session Two is not to dwell on how traumatized you were as a child or how difficult your life has been since then. Your work is to realize that beneath all your pain is a joyful child who is now eager to emerge from a self-protective ego cocoon. Your general assignment, therefore, is to give that child all the love that you feel it needs in order to allow this metamorphosis to occur.

To do this assignment, you must have first come to a place of choice—an inner sense that you have the freedom to actually choose to be your authentic self. But bear in mind that there's a paradox involved: You can't access this place of choice until you have *compassion for the choices you've already made.* So where, you might ask, does this compassion come from?

First, realize that there is no one to blame for your pain, not even you! You confined yourself in this cocoon *to survive unbearable psychic pain.* It was an unavoidable choice, the only choice you could have made. It's now time to value the truth of your decisions, to respect the choices you could not help but make, and to accept the inevitable consequences. In the processing of choosing to survive, you lost your true self. That's just what happened.

Second, notice the recurring patterns in your quest to find yourself. See them *as groping attempts to heal the unresolved psychic pain you have carried since childhood.* At this point the key question has become: What have you learned about love in this long and painful process? What insights have you gained?

You have been re-creating stale versions of your original wounding childhood relationships; without insight, you are doomed to continue this melodrama. But insight brings compassion and the ability to recognize these choices as part of a meaningful quest.

Now, with these two points in mind, take the time to examine each significant relationship and event in your Life Chart. Review them from this positive and compassionate perspective, and write down your thoughts and feelings in your sacred journal. But instead of looking at an event or relationship as *merely* painful, traumatic, or devastating, ask yourself these four questions:

1. How can I see this relationship or event as an effort to find love, healing, and resolution?

In truth, such an effort is the hidden logic behind all of our choices. We are always trying to find love and healing and to avoid unbearable psychic pain. (At least we think it's unbearable.) Of course, now you know that not only can you bear it, but you can feel all the way through it to the joy on the other side. Write your answer to this question in your journal.

> *2. Now ask yourself: In those relationships that repeat the patterns of my original trauma, what have I been choosing up to now? To go through the pain? Or to numb it out?*

If you've chosen to numb it out, that means *the original pain is still there.* You must instead connect the pain to the child within, and feel through it. Until now you've likely been making the same choice that your child made long ago: to check out and shut down; you are still frozen in that place of no-choice. Recognizing the patterns I'm describing here is the first step to a place of choice. Think about these patterns and record them in your sacred journal.

> *3. Also ask yourself: Which key people from my childhood (parents, siblings, or other figures) remind me of the key people in my present life?*

You have very likely re-created in your *present* life the crucial relationship scenarios from your past. Where are you now stuck emotionally, and why? Record your answers.

Here's some help on answering this one: Suppose that as a child you had an emotionally unavailable parent whom you deeply loved. Because you couldn't know why your parent was unavailable, you would naturally turn the experience of rejection into a story that says "being me is not enough" or "there must be something wrong with me." As a result, your serious relationships in later life would likely be with emotionally unavailable partners similar to that parent; this would become your intuitive choice. You would choose these sorts of partners, first, because of an unconscious wish to finally heal that wound and, second, because that is where you are stuck in your understanding, or your *truth,* of relationships and love.

Your "truth" is whatever you have learned so far from what you have experienced in your life. It consists of whatever you received from your partners in relationship until you break that pattern by actually loving yourself.

So write down your truth as you see it now; record everything that you can in your journal about your current relationships and how they relate to your lifelong quest to find yourself.

For example, one of my clients was a woman from Peru who had been sexually abused as a child. Her father would leave her at his parents' house, where she was sexually molested by an uncle. Desperately wanting to escape her painful childhood memories, she moved to America. Yet, as an adult in America, she unwittingly re-created every significant family relationship from her childhood. One friend was just like her critical mother. Another was like her grandmother, who had loved her the most as a child. She also became involved with an emotionally unavailable man like her father. This man repeatedly triggered in her the deep feelings of aloneness she had experienced when her father would leave her at his parents' house. Like most of us, she unerringly re-created the relationship patterns that existed when she emotionally shut down as a child.

What is the unconscious intention behind this uncanny phenomenon?

I believe our hidden purpose is revealed in our need to face again the traumas that have wounded us. We are seeking a new and different choice for life and love. By re-enacting early relationships, we are aiming to triumph and heal ourselves. In other words, we re-create these wounding childhood scenarios so that we can finally, and decisively, defeat the fear that originally defeated us. By succeeding, we recover the sense of innate value that we lost and finally experience that *who we are is enough!*

But there is yet another dynamic at play. We not only pick partners who resemble key figures from our childhoods; we also pick partners who mirror to us the issues we are currently struggling with. Consider the person you are now in a relationship with, or the last person with whom you had a relationship. Chances are this person is struggling with the same issues and fears as you (and probably also resembles, emotionally if not physically, a significant figure from your childhood). Now, ask yourself the following question, and record your answers in your sacred journal.

4. Is the significant person in my life like me emotionally? Are the issues that we both struggle with similar or somehow complementary?

As we have seen, in your inner quest to find yourself, you are externalizing that quest in the form of your partner. We all pick partners who match our hidden, internal psychic structure. Why? Because we are looking outside ourselves (Stage Five in the Cycle of Life) for something that is already inside. Until we have fully surrendered to love, we are continually externalizing our inner quest!

When you can see the lost child inside your partner and can recognize on some level that you are both struggling with the same issues and are on the same quest, you've taken a significant step toward finding the person you *really* want—the lost child *inside* of you! The purpose of the Life Chart is to help you to finally *internalize* the quest. Then you won't have to go outside yourself in search of yourself anymore. So go ahead and explore in your sacred journal why you have set up every relationship and how every relationship is related to your quest.

Here's a little bit of additional coaching: As you do this thorough review of your Life Chart, begin to take total accountability for your choices. You can do this by accepting and embracing all of these events and relationships *without being a victim or denying the love that you have felt*. This is just a beginning. We will explore this practice in the next chapter.

If you have thoroughly answered the questions in this chapter, you will now be in a place of choice. Decide now to choose to be your true self, rather than the false self you created to be accepted and loved. This is what I mean when I say, "It's your turn!"

In fact, it is always your turn if you're willing to choose it! You become willing to take your turn when you realize you'll never be happy living out other people's dreams. It is only by going through the black hole of pain to embrace and heal the child within yourself that you find the courage to live your dreams. My job is to show you how living your dreams *is a choice that you can now make.* And that your greatest dream is to be your authentic self!

By doing this work, you'll begin to encounter synchronistic or serendipitous events that will help you move forward. These events are "electrifying signs" telling you you're on the right path, that you've re-ignited your connection to the Unified Field. The whole universe begins to say "Yes!" to you, whereas before you were saying no to yourself. You are now on board the "Real You Express," whose destination is your joyful place in this loving plan. One of my clients wrote this poem for me after his sessions. It's in fact called the "The Real You Express":

> This is about a child who gave himself away.
> He became an adult, never able to play.
> He wore a facade to hide his fears.
> Time slipped away, and so did the years.
> Then in the perfect order, at just the right time,

A teacher appeared, a coach by design.
"Give me your hand, walk into your fears.
You'll find the answers that will bring your tears.
It is truly a ride on the road to success."
He said, "It's your turn on the Real You Express.
Look into the past. Write down your dreams.
Allow yourself to surrender. Just feel what that means.
The little child is lonely and waiting inside
To experience love and laughter, no longer to hide.
It's time to be truthful and feel despair.
No matter how long it takes, you must go there.
Right on the other side are the feelings of joy,
The heightened awareness of a lost little boy.
Hold onto your heart and let the love inside.
The truth shall be yours. It's quite a ride.
Your life begins to sparkle, you'll feel so blessed.
Then comes the realization of the Real You Express."

—Wil Tarnofsky

Homework:

The homework for Session Two is to share your Life Chart—and the insights and compassion you have gained by answering the questions in this chapter—with at least three people *with whom there is some risk in doing so.* By this I mean that the thought of sharing might make you nervous, even afraid. Of course, don't share where you feel there may be literally disastrous consequences, where what is shared might risk harm to you or others. Use your discretion, but press beyond your comfort zone.

The principle of opening up the cocoon of your consciousness is: *Until I let somebody in, I can't come out.* You entered this cocoon to be safe, and to keep others out. This cocoon was born from the belief that who you are is not enough! So opening your cocoon and inviting significant others to come in is a very important step. This homework begins the process of letting others into your cocoon to the point where you realize you no longer need it. For during this process you will touch people deeply with the story of your quest and begin to realize that being you is not only enough but also beautiful and inspirational. Even more important are the feelings of compassion you will begin to feel for yourself and your journey toward self-discovery. Preferably, share your Life Chart with at least one parental figure. And share everything, in detail.

Here's some extra coaching to bear in mind while doing your Session Two homework: The story of your

quest is your best attempt to make sense of the predicament in which you found yourself. What you
are doing in this homework is simply telling your story
to people—perhaps your mother, father, or siblings—
who may not know you have a story of such profundity. In sharing your quest, you may find out about
other parts of your story that you never knew. For
example, you may be suprised to discover that there
was more love in your life than you realized; or, you
may find that perhaps things were not exactly the way
they seemed. Or, you may see more clearly how much
of your childhood pain occurred as a result of your
unconscious recoil from love in reaction to wounds
you received.

Many clients have done this exercise with amazing results. Sharing a Life Chart with our parents can
let us know of past events that we've been unaware of.
Many parents express the profound wish that they had
known of these traumas so that they could have "been
there" for the child they loved. It is often the walls we
have put up to protect ourselves that separate us from
the love and acceptance we so desperately want.

The Life Chart of a married client of mine
included an affair that she had never told her husband
about. Understandably petrified by the prospect of
sharing her chart with her husband, she decided to
bring him to a session and share the chart with him in
my office. When he understood the true nature and
perspective of the Life Chart in general, and her life-
patterns in particular, her husband understood the

affair as it related to her childhood wounds and the emotional pain she had carried ever since. He did not fall apart or withdraw his love. Sharing the chart with him actually strengthened their intimacy!

If you share your Life Chart fearlessly you will begin to see through the fears and illusions that you have allowed to stand in your way. For you *will* face and move through your fears as you share your chart. That's part of its purpose. You can't really know that your fears are illusions until you actually face them, feel them, and go through them.

Before you do your homework and go on to the next chapter, read the wonderful story below by Pema Chodron. It will give you the formula for defeating fear.

Overcoming Fear

(**F**alse **E**xaggerations **A**ppearing **R**eal)

Once there was a young warrior. Her teacher told her that she had to do battle with fear. She didn't want to do that. It seemed too aggressive; it was scary; it seemed unfriendly. But the teacher said she had to do it, and gave her the instructions for the battle. The day arrived. The student stood on one side, and fear stood on the other. The warrior was feeling very small, and fear was looking big and wrathful. They both had their weapons. The young warrior roused herself and went toward fear, prostrated three times, and asked, "May I have permission to go into battle with you?"

Fear said, "Thank you for showing me so much respect that you ask permission."

Then the young warrior asked, "How can I defeat you?"

Fear replied, "My weapons are that I talk fast, and I get very close to your face. Then you get completely un-nerved, and you do whatever I say. If you don't do what I tell you, I have no power. You can listen to me, and you can have respect for me. You can even be convinced by me. But if you don't do what I say, I have no power."

In that way, the student warrior learned how to defeat fear.[1]

Allen's Story

Facing My Deepest Fear

As you will see on your Life Chart, every relationship plays its part in the journey to finally embrace yourself. This has certainly been true for me. Every relationship in my life has been a gift on my journey back to my authentic self and my original state of soul consciousness. But in the case of Rachel, it was a revelation and a profound lesson in the importance of letting go as well as taking hold. Rachel's story also illustrates to me that the soul contains the events that shall befall it and that these events-to-come are often revealed in dreams and synchronistic episodes. My romance with Rachel was the one relationship that led me to confront my deepest terror and fear and finally fully surrender to my deeper joy, intention, and purpose. All these amazing factors entered into this dramatic relationship with Rachel. I am sure that there are equally important relationships on your Life Chart, if you are able to see them as gifts.

In 1989 I was living on a horse ranch in Sonoma, California, preparing myself to return to private practice after an eight-year sabbatical in the nonprofit sector. Suddenly one night I had a dream that I was making love with a small, beautiful redhead named Rachel. There was nothing but joy and laughter in this dream, and although I knew no one by the name of Rachel, I woke up knowing this dream was important. I remember telling my housemate about the dream and mentioning that I was sure I would meet this person soon.

Two weeks later, I was sharing at a Sunday church service and afterward people were hugging and embracing each other—as was the custom at this church. At one point, I walked up to a young lady with two beautiful twin daughters and hugged her. It was instant chemistry. I walked away, then came back and hugged her again. This time I also softly kissed her and asked her what her name was. She told me it was Rachel—and she was a small, beautiful redhead, just like the woman in my dream!

We made a date to get together, and within two weeks we were literally living my dream. Just as the dream indicated, there was nothing but joy and laughter in our relationship; Rachel and I just could not see enough of each other! I would wake up in the morning with Rachel, and her twin daughters would leap into bed with us. The girls were nine years old, and they and I quickly connected at a very deep level because we were all twins.

I was keenly aware that I was loving and being loved at a profound and joyful level, and I fully surrendered to it. Rachel used to say to me, "Allen, I'm scared to death of how deep this relationship is." And I would reply, "Rachel, I'm just a little less scared than you."

Before I go any further, I should mention that twins are both blessed and haunted by the deep intimacy and love they have shared with each other. Not many people are able to allow themselves to explore the realms of intimacy that twins feel so deeply in the womb and as children. The reason Rachel was allowing herself to be loved that deeply by me was that she was loving and being loved just as deeply by her identical twin daughters.

Elsewhere in this book I tell the story of how my mother revealed, much later in my life, that I was not wanted in the womb. In a deep sense, all I had to hold onto as an infant was my twin brother. I was born two minutes before him and undoubtedly experienced a moment of panic or terror when we separated. I had never consciously felt this terror, but I definitely had fears of deep intimacy and abandonment as a younger man, and I had certainly experienced it in my last marriage.

In Rachel, I believe, I subconsciously manifested a relationship with someone I was able to love as deeply and joyfully as I had my twin. Rachel was therefore someone who could also eventually lead me to my deepest terror and aloneness—which she certainly did.

About six months into our relationship, things began to happen. Rachel flunked her teacher's exam twice and went into a deep place of unworthiness and self-hatred. She began to push me away and close off to protect herself, for I am sure she was convinced I would reject her. After a few weeks of this, I suggested that we not see each other for a month and then get together when she was ready to see me again.

A few weeks later, one of the twins called and invited me to come by the house to pick up some tickets for a play that she and her sister were in. When I dropped by, they were all there, and my love for them had not skipped a beat. I hugged them all, and my heart was totally open, for I had truly missed them. I asked Rachel to go out for dinner, and she agreed to get together with me the following Friday.

As I left her house that morning, I remember realizing that I had not held back any feelings my heart was still completely open. But the next day I received a message from Rachel on my answering machine. She had decided she was not ready to see me again and was canceling our date. I left a message on her machine that I was disappointed but that I would still attend the twins' play.

That night as I sat on my couch, I realized that it was time for me to let go. I knew part of Rachel really loved me, but I also knew another part of her was scared to death and there was no way I could convince her to go beyond her fears. I went to bed that night not denying my deep love for Rachel and not feeling like a victim about letting go of the relationship. I was ready to let go!

In the middle of the night I suddenly woke up in a state of stark terror! I had never experienced anything like what I was feeling at that time—an incredible sense of desperation and panic. I could hardly breathe and was literally gasping for breath.

I totally surrendered to the terror and fell on the bed completely drained. The terror lasted about one minute, but it was a minute I will never forget!

I looked at the clock. It was 1:10AM. My mind became completely clear as to what I had experienced. I realized that I had just re-experienced the moment of terror I had felt when I was separated at birth from my twin. I had loved Rachel as deeply as my twin; otherwise, I would not have felt this same terror. I also understood that I could now either fully take hold or let go in this relationship, because I was no longer afraid of the terror that had always been there. I knew I could now love that deeply without any fear.

I also felt a growing sense of inner excitement because I knew that underneath my deepest pain was joy—and I had just surrendered to what was obviously my deepest terror. It should come as no surprise that this incident is at the root of many of the discoveries I am sharing with you in this book.

I called Rachel the next morning, told her what had happened, and thanked her for being honest. I thanked her because her honesty had given me the opportunity to feel something I never knew was there—the terror of my original separation from my twin during the birth trauma. I also told her I could now either take hold or let go in our relationship. She again told me that she was not ready to see me.

It really did not matter to me now because I knew I had just gone through an inner door. A powerful sense of joy and excitement was already welling up in me. And it had nothing to do with Rachel.

From this point, events in my life moved rapidly. I was on the Express! Within a week, I had an appointment with Linda, a massage practitioner who had been referred to me by a stranger. The moment Linda touched me on the massage table, I went right into the womb. All the joyful sensory memories and deep intimacy I had shared with my twin, in utero, were now available to me, and I totally surrendered to them. Linda facilitated this process by enacting the role of my twin.

At the end of that session, which lasted over three hours, she said, "Allen, you and your twin were literally one." Now I knew I was really onto something, and I was determined to surrender completely in this free fall into joy and bliss.

In the next session, I again went into the womb, but this time went beyond my twin to a full experience of myself and my own uniqueness as distinct from my twin. It was during this session that I began to feel a deep sense of intention and purpose that almost propelled me off the table.

In my last session with Linda—and there were only three—I told her I was going all the way. I knew there was nothing to be afraid of, and I totally surrendered to the experience. In that session, I was definitely in contact with people I had loved deeply in my life who had passed on, people such as my grandfather, my maid Delia, and my beloved mentor Grace Petitclerc. I was literally dancing on the table in joy. At the end of the session, I leaped off the table—stark naked—and announced to Linda from a place of joy: "Linda, I am totally in touch with my deepest joy, intention, and purpose!"

Linda told me that she had spent most of the session dancing around the table, and when I asked her how she felt, she said, "I feel like I was kissed by God."

I had obviously tapped into the spring of joy beneath my well of grief and terror. I was re-entering my original state of soul consciousness (the Unified Field)—and soon my whole life began to reflect this momentous experience.

Rapidly, my re-entry manifested itself in my music, my acting, my friendships, and especially my work. In going through my deepest terror, I was expanding into my deeper joy. Within a few weeks, my client load increased threefold, and my clients were able to complete their work with me in seven two-hour sessions. For the single most effective gift I gave them—and continue to give them—is that of sharing the joy of being truly honest and of being myself and seeing the joy beneath their pain. By doing so, I inspire my clients to go through their fears and find this same joy within themselves. (It's interesting that most of the people who are directed to me have had significant birth trauma or separation early in childhood.)

Let's look at my story as an excellent example of how our lives are divinely guided and how we are pulled from within to surrender to what is deepest within us. As I said, the soul contains the events that shall befall it, and my dream of Rachel was clearly a message from my soul telling me about my next step. We all have access to this inner guidance or call if we will but listen and respond, as I did. I have listened and responded many times in my life, and I have never been let down.

It's all about love and surrendering to love. My whole life has been a quest to feel and love as deeply as I did as a child. In loving Rachel as deeply as my twin, I was, in reality, loving myself by allowing myself to feel that deeply.

Great love can both take hold and let go. In letting go of Rachel—not as a victim, and not denying the love—I was finally and fully embracing myself and returning to my original connection to the Unified Field of love and soul consciousness.

There are no accidents. I am fully aware that once we surrender to this deep inner pull and call, people and events occur that are all gifts on our inner journey to unity and fulfillment. Rachel was not an accident. She was an incredible gift on my path, and I surrendered to it. Linda was not an accident either. She was the one person who would allow me to do what I needed and not be trapped by her own fear—and she was referred to me by a complete stranger. This is Einstein's "spooky stuff operating at a distance." In reality, it is a loving plan in action, which manifests itself to each of us every day—if we have the courage to listen and respond.

And now do you have the courage to listen and respond?

12

taking accountability for your life

session three

Now you've seen your whole life as a quest to open your heart and discover who you really are. You've understood and have had compassion for the fact that the child inside you has been hard at work for years, re-enacting in your relationships the original wounding childhood scenarios. And you now realize that you set up these relationships in order to resolve and heal the place where you were wounded, where you emotionally checked out and became stuck. Finally, it all makes sense!

From this new perspective of compassionate understanding, it's time to begin the essential process of forgiving yourself for the painful choices you made before you knew better. By understanding and fully forgiving yourself, you will come to a new level of healing and a new place of inner validation. And you'll also be able to start forgiving others for the choices they made.

It's time to stop being a victim. It's time to start forgiving yourself and others. It's time to open your heart. It's time for *action*!

So here is your first assignment in Session Three:

Make a list of five or six key people in your life toward whom you have feelings of anger or resentment.

This list might include your mother, father, sister, brother, and friend, former lovers. But there's one requirement: The last person on your list must be *you*. This requisite shouldn't come as a surprise. Consider the many reasons you may feel resentment toward yourself: shutting yourself off from others, and probably from many opportunities for love; surrendering to fear and sealing yourself in a confining, self-protective cocoon; abandoning your true self and becoming an artificial entity in order to receive other people's conditional love and approval. No wonder you feel resentment! *You may have never taken your turn!* How could you *not* be carrying some resentment toward yourself?

So, go ahead, be honest with yourself, make the list of these people—and write their names into your sacred journal. You will be working with them in this session.

The lists of key people that my clients create, by the way, almost always include their mothers.

All parents make mistakes; but our mothers, who bear the greater burden in raising us, have many more opportunities to seemingly fail us than anyone else in our lives. Seeing that mothers are human, and live on this unhealed planet—and can give us only what they have received—we can safely assume that your mother "failed" you in some way and will probably be on your list.

With your list in hand, you are now going to do a two-step internal cleansing that involves working with your resentments. Start by using my suggestions in Chapter 9 about creating a sacred space and preparing yourself to do this kind of profound inner work. Once you've prepped yourself in this way, you are ready to begin this two-part exercise.

The Cleansing Exercise: Part 1

Address each person on your list—just as if that person were actually with you; express out loud all the resentments you hold against that person.

Do this with total feeling and conviction, and from a victim's point of view. Formulate your resentments into statements or accusations that begin with the word "You." These might be statements such as:

- "You made me feel alone!"
- "You never cared about my feelings!"
- "You were never emotionally available for me."
- "You were cruel and unloving!"

– "You made me feel guilty!"

– "You abused me physically and emotionally!"

The statements might also include specific events of extreme physical, emotional, and sexual abuse.

These are statements that express in essence "You made me feel . . ." or "You did . . ."

You can do this exercise sitting down, standing up, pacing around, whatever allows you to tune into and fully express these long-pent-up feelings. Go full-throttle into the victim state. Don't hold back. Express these resentments out loud and by yourself. If it helps, set a chair in front of you and imagine the person is facing you. Go through your list and let each person have it with both barrels! Let it rip! It may become quite heavy—and that's okay and quite natural. You are dredging up and releasing emotions you've held inside, often for many years. So do it—out loud!

Do these people one by one. Did you notice how *heavy* it feels to be a victim? Of course it does, because you've been carrying or dragging this heavy resentment baggage your whole life and you've probably manifested it in every key love relationship you've had.

After you have done Part 1 with each person, immediately go to Part 2.

The Cleansing Exercise: Part 2

You've fully expressed your resentments toward each of the significant people in your life. Now it's time to turn it completely around! This time, take full accountability for your own feelings using "I" statements. Go at it one person at a time, and with the same list of people.

Part 2 is about taking responsibility for choices you have made with these people; it's about being accountable for the consequences of holding onto these feelings for as long as you have.

I don't want you to issue accusations as you did in the last part. Instead you're going to proclaim your own accountability for your feelings, actions, and inner experience. And as your victim statements in Part 1 emphasized the word "you," these statements should emphasize the word "I." Here are some examples:

- "Mother, I chose to withdraw from the world in response to my feelings toward you."

- "Mother/father/other, I realize that you treated me the way you did because you closed your heart and checked out in response to your own unbearable psychic pain. But I am the one who felt unloved, closed my heart, and emotionally checked out of my life."

- "I am the one who turned away from my authentic self and became someone else in order to get attention."

- "I am the one who chose to push people away from me and to withhold the full, honest expression of my deepest feelings and self."

- "I am the one who chose to withhold my feelings of love for you."

— "I am the one who decided that being
   me was not enough."

— "I am the one who went through my
   life manifesting people like you and
   re-creating my relationship with you,
   because that's where I was stuck!"—
   and so on.

In this way, complete with each person by taking accountability for your past behavior. Did you notice how *light* being accountable feels, compared with how heavy it felt being a victim?

Regardless of what anyone said to you or did to you, you alone made the decision to close your heart and bury your deepest feelings. This courageous act of taking accountability for your own pain and resentment is a key step toward finally surrendering to your deepest innate urge to love and unite with others.

Here are a few important tips to keep in mind when doing Part 2:

— Do not say things that are not really true
   for you.

— Don't use my words as an automatic script.

— Find what feels true for you and speak
   your unique truths.

— Do not let yourself off the hook. Don't
   slide backward and continue to blame
   others for feelings that you felt and
   decisions that you alone have made.

— Examine as deeply as you can how you
have related to the people on your list
and what choices you have made. Be as
clear as possible about what you chose
to do, so that you can truly take account-
bility for your life. To the degree that
you don't do this, you will continue to
live as a victim, with all of the negative
consequences that come with this role.

— Cover every issue and incident that you
expressed the first time around from a
victim state. Don't leave anything out;
work with each issue until you have
turned it around.

— Remember that reading these words
is not a magic formula! Your full and
authentic participation is required.

— You may need to do this process more
than once, and perhaps over time, with
the particularly difficult issues. You will
feel it inside when you have released
something. The feeling of lightness,
freedom, and new energy is the sign
you are on the right track.

Having now completed this part of the Cleansing
Exercise, there is one last assignment:

*Address each person on your list and declare that you
are now taking full accountability for your feelings and the
decisions you made in your life.*

This exercise is a prelude to this chapter's homework—it's a rehearsal of sorts. For this exercise, use
some version of the following words with the people
on your list:

— "Mother (or whoever), I realize you are not responsible for feelings that I felt and decisions that I alone made as a child (or in our relationship). Until now I have been holding you responsible, but I now take full accountability for what is mine."

— "Life sent you to me exactly as you were so that I could learn the lessons I have learned, come to this new place of choice, and open my heart again. You are life's gift to me, and I love you."

— "The biggest gift I can give to you and to myself is the full, open, honest, and free expression of who I really am regardless of the risks to our relationship."

— "It is more important that I love myself and be who I am than that you love me for being who I am not."

Again, this is not a mandatory script. If it seems true for you, feel free to use it. Otherwise, find and speak the truths you need to speak in order to take full accountability in these relationships. And speak them out loud with total conviction and feeling. See how it feels to be accountable versus being a victim? It feels good, doesn't it? Own this feeling!

Taking total accountability for your own feelings and choices in life is a crucial step toward recovering your original state of soul consciousness. It is also important for you to realize that your relationships with these people were painful *because* you really loved them, and that you were willing to do anything—even deny your true self—to receive their love! All your choices, even the most painful ones, revolved around love; to recognize this is to recognize that the driving force in you—your true nature—is (what else?) love.

Allow me to elaborate for a moment on why we do the Cleansing Exercise.

This cleansing gives a voice to two aspects of the child within you. Part 1 gives a voice to the wounded child who fled from unbearable pain, and away from love, into a cocoon of safety. Part 2 gives a voice to the soul-conscious child who has been guiding your journey back to love. The child within you knows it has checked out, and it needs to express both its resentment and pain and its accountability for the choices it made. So in this exercise you are giving all parts of this inner child an authentic voice.

Making the "I" statements in Part 2 is the first step toward taking total accountability for your life. It also allows you to fully connect with the deepest part of yourself. (By the way, this place within you also will feel compassion for those many people in your life who *also* checked out and cut themselves off from love!)

In doing this exercise for myself, I realized that my own mother behaved the way she did with me because she was a very sad person who felt cut off from love. Unfortunately, she was unable to see that this was her choice, so she carried her resentment to the end of her life. I understood that there was a lost child within her who never had a voice. I could not change who she was or how she had been. But I came to a place of compassionate understanding that allowed me to love her as she was and to see that *she was in fact life's gift to me exactly as she was.* She truly did the best she could at the time, given the choices she had made and what had happened to her.

Finding compassion for these people in your life is very important. But remember, compassion begins with you! And once you fully love yourself, this love must be extended to others in order to be kept alive. By feeling compassion both for yourself and for others, it becomes easier to take full accountability for your own life and your choices. And that is the direct route back to your original, authentic self. You can't make the transition from ego consciousness to soul consciousness by being a victim and denying love.

With all this in mind, you are now ready for a small but important concluding exercise:

Declare out loud, "I will never say no to my authentic self again or allow myself to be controlled by fear."

Write this statement down, keep it close to you, and repeat it often to yourself.

As you will read in the story following this chapter, I made that statement to myself with total conviction in 1987. After doing so, my life dramatically changed . Within one week I had verified my Unified Field theory, and my part in this ever-evolving loving plan became crystal clear. Subsequent events quickly propelled me to a place where I had to take full responsibility for this knowledge and for what I deeply know and feel—as I am doing with you now.

So, you have gone through this Cleansing Exercise (also known as the "victim/accountability" exercise) with five or six key people, including yourself. Having done this emotional cleansing, it is now time to complete your self-forgiveness work. Here's what I would like you to do:

Take out and look over your Life Chart once again. Remind yourself of the victim-based beliefs and feelings that resulted from the relationships that caused you pain. And remember: In your former role of victim, you believed that your pain was created by outside forces. You learned to externalize psychic pain in order to protect yourself from pain that may *still* seem unbearable. You cannot change what you did in the past for the sake of your emotional survival. But you *can* change what you will do and how you will regard yourself in the future.

That's why I want you to forgive yourself for the choices you made that are recorded in your Life Chart. Do this in the knowledge that the universe forgives you totally, and unconditionally!

So here is the exercise that allows you to complete this work of forgiving yourself.

Say out loud to yourself, "I forgive myself for all that I have done to survive and for the past which I cannot change. And now I have another choice!"

Forgive yourself, and mean it! Once you do this, you will truly see that your life has been a quest to become whole and take your rightful place in this loving plan, rather than an ongoing and pointless struggle to survive. Your Life Chart will help you see this quest more clearly as you will begin to understand and feel greater compassion for yourself.

Homework:

The homework for this session is to take accountability for your life by literally contacting all of the people on your list (those who are still alive and can be contacted) and expressing your new intentions.

You may contact them in person, or by phone. When you speak to them, use the following accountability statements as a guide. Proceed through each statment in the order provided below.

1. "_____ [name of the person], I've been holding some resentment toward a few people in my life, including you. However, it is really resentment toward myself for blaming others for my inability to take risks, express my deepest feelings, and ask for what I really want."

2. "I no longer hold you responsible for feelings that I felt and decisions that I alone made as a child (or in our relationship)."

3. "How can I blame you or hold you responsible for decisions that I alone made?"

4. "I now fully accept you, exactly as you are, and I know that you have always been a gift that life has given me."

5. "The biggest gift I can give you is the full, free, and honest expression of my deepest feelings, regardless of the risk to our relationship; doing this is an act of love."

6. "It is more important now that I love myself for who I really am than that I try to become someone else to earn your love."

In sum and substance, make these six statements in sequence, clearly and deliberately.

As you talk with each person, be sure to *not* speak from a victim standpoint. Just be fully present and focus on taking accountability for your life and all the elements of the relationship. Remember, you are not doing this to make them feel guilty or to suggest any blame for your experiences. Remain very conscious, and don't let yourself slip unwittingly back into the victim/blaming role.

If your listener begins to speak before you are finished, stop them gently. Tell them that, for the sake of your own happiness and peace of mind, you need to take full accountability for the choices you've made in your life. Let them know that you are not expressing these things to make them feel bad or guilty in any way; assure them you are doing this for *you* and for your relationship with them.

If you speak from a place of understanding and are fully present with them, they'll get it. If, after you've spoken your truth, they wish to say something, let them speak. Listen with your full presence.

Taking full responsibility for the decisions you made to avoid pain allows your heart to open. You are now healing yourself! All my clients who have been healed have healed themselves. When you have fulfilled this exercise, you will have come to a new place of choice because you will have faced your deepest wounds, taken full responsibility for them, and chosen forgiveness instead of ongoing anger and resentment.

From now on, you can say yes to your true self. You can express your deepest feelings whenever you need to. You no longer need to be controlled by fear or by your need for outer validation. You can now choose to be guided by inner validation.

The greatest joy in life is knowing that you are part of something vastly greater than yourself, and that you are playing your part in it. This far surpasses the joy even of having a great relationship with someone you love very deeply. This *is* what you came here to do—to play your part in a grand loving plan, not to invest all the love and meaning you have in one person. You are here to give the gift of yourself to life by opening your heart and radiating your true self to everyone you meet! When you can do this, your very presence will facilitate change, and ego effort will no longer be necessary. This transformation really begins when you take accountability for all of your choices, as you have now done in Session Three.

Remember:

— "Peace begins with me."

— "Love begins with me."

— "Gratitude begins with me."

— "Joy begins with me."

— "Understanding begins with me."

— "Compassion begins with me."

The Fort Mason Story

Walking into a Precognitive Vision

*There is always one moment
in childhood when the door
opens and lets the future in.*

—Graham Greene

I remember one such moment as a child.

It was a precognitive vision I had when I was six years old, a vision that appeared to me after I was taken away from my beloved grandfather. In this vision, I saw a great bridge painted orange—right in the middle of the picture—with some water on one side and some houses on the other. Sunlight was reflecting off both in a very particular way. Later I was to discover that this was the Golden Gate Bridge. It was not a dream but a clear and lucid vision.

I was a small boy, and I was drowning in the depths of my despair; I was in the midst of closing my heart and retiring into a self-protective cocoon of fear and ego consciousness—for I had just been taken away from my grandfather. Yet in a transcendent moment of time, I was granted a vision of where I would be one day when I was able to see, once again, through the eyes of that beautiful, alive, and loving child who was sadly now going into ego consciousness.

Amazingly, this event took place in New-tonville, Massachusetts. I had never been west of Massachusetts, so I had no idea what the San Francisco Bay Area or even the Golden Gate Bridge looked like.

As I grew older, I never forgot that vision, but I couldn't draw an exact picture of it. All I really knew was that the Golden Gate Bridge was in the middle and it had something to do with my destiny.

Well, sure enough, my destiny led me to San Francisco, where I was stationed as a Navy pilot from 1959 to 1962. There, I soon met Karen, the woman with whom (as you know from earlier in this book) I finally opened my heart and fully felt the heights of my original joy and the depths of my repressed childhood pain. After my dramatic encounter with her, I felt sure that my precognitive vision was telling me that San Francisco was to be an important part of my destiny. Up to that time, it certainly had been. So I dismissed this vision of my destiny as having already been fulfilled.

But that vision, that moment, was to be part of something far more profound and illuminating.

By 1979 I had written the first draft of my Unified Field theory, but I had not yet proven to myself that love—and not light—was the overrid-ing constant of the universe. I knew Einstein was correct in terms of what science could see through its limited consciousness but wrong in terms of what can be perceived and experienced from the standpoint of the within of things. And it was obvious to me that extra-sensory or paranormal events illustrated a different relation to time and space.

For example, in scientific terms, precognition (the perception of a future event before it occurs) is considered possible. But it would mean that signals or information of some kind could travel backward in time which, according to special relativity, would be particles going faster than light.

But with the acceptance of the existence of the Unified Field of love—a psychic energy field within which time and space do not exist—the effect would be the same but the cause would be due to forces beyond the physical realm.

As such, precognition would fit comfortably into established physics and would also explain why it is experienced mainly between people who have deep loving connections, such as lovers, mates, and mothers and their children.

So in 1979, I knew that this Unified Field was the one constant of the universe, but I had no direct experience of it as existing beyond time and space. And until I did, it could be only a theory.

As a result, I left my private practice and went into the nonprofit sector, where I concentrated on empowering people within the organizations to which I was attached. For eight years, I concentrated on marketing and development within these organizations. But I had a nagging sense deep inside that there was something else I really wanted to do.

By 1987, I was one of five administrators at Sonoma Valley Hospital, yet I still had that nagging feeling. One of my close friends, who was the top administrator at the hospital, took a five-day self-awareness seminar in San Francisco and returned with a more joyful and positive attitude toward life.

I immediately decided I needed to deal with some issues in my own life. I was still being somewhat careful. I was not fully saying yes to myself, and I still had some old childhood resentment and victim issues that were getting in my way.

So I took the five-day basic training seminar that my friend had just completed.

During that seminar, I experienced the victim accountability exercise that you just completed. The power of this exercise literally changed my life.

I completely surrendered to this exercise and noticed dramatically how light and powerful I felt being totally accountable as opposed to how heavy and powerless I felt being a victim. I also realized that taking full accountability for my life was really saying yes to myself, something I had not yet fully done.

At that moment, I literally pulled an internal switch and openly declared: "I will never say no to myself again or allow myself to be controlled by fear!"

Well, the universe must have been waiting for me to fully say yes to myself, because the series of highly synchronistic events that happened in the next five days were certainly no accident. Not only did these events prove to me that our lives are divinely guided and that we are all connected at the heart level, but they also led me to the proof that

I had been seeking: that within a state of soul consciousness there is no time and space and that love is the sole constant of the universe.

On the last evening of the seminar, I made the decision to take the advanced training course, which started the following Wednesday. My personal goal during the advanced training was to reconnect with my original childhood state of soul consciousness. I knew I was now fully in touch with the child within me, and I was no longer afraid to say yes to myself.

During the first day of the training, we were asked to form small groups in which we would relate to each other from our intuitive feelings.

During the group, someone suddenly pointed at me and said, "You've been sitting on something for over eight years. When are you going to own it?"

He was right. I had been sitting on my Unified Field theory for more than eight years and had not fully owned it. This person was a total stranger and knew absolutely nothing about me, but I got the message. The universe was telling me it was time to own my theory, and I knew it, too.

The sessions went from noon to midnight and were very intense. The next day, about halfway through the session, we were asked to form a large circle and then walk across the room to the person directly opposite. That person would be our buddy for the next three days, and it was important that we be there for each other.

Seemingly by accident—and remember there

are no accidents when you are on this path—the person directly opposite me in that room of over a hundred people was a lovely young lady named Janet Belias. As Janet and I exchanged small talk, I told her I had almost fallen asleep at the wheel of my car driving the fifty miles home to Sonoma from San Francisco the previous evening. She told me that she lived in San Francisco and would have me stay at her place but that it was just a studio and almost too cramped even for just her. She also mentioned she had some friends who lived in the city who might put me up.

Before she even finished, I said emphatically, "I have to stay at your place." I said this from a place of deep intention and knowing.

At first, she was upset, then clearly saw there was nothing romantic about my request and intention. Sensing my innocence, she said it was okay.

The soul contains the events that shall befall it; I knew from somewhere deep inside that I had to stay at her home and I was not about to say no to myself.

We went to her house very late that evening. The next morning we remembered that the day's exercise was to come in dressed opposite the way we usually dressed.

For no known reason, I had packed some old, dirty clothes, even though I knew nothing about the exercise, further confirming that I was in a place of surrender and totally trusting my intuition and inner guidance.

I told Janet that I wanted to cover myself with

dirt and be filthy, since I am usually quite neat, and asked her if there was some place close by where I could find some dirt. She told me that we were only two blocks away from Fort Mason Park and that she had seen some mounds of dirt in the parking lot there the day before.

Her apartment was on Octavia Street, the only street in San Francisco that runs directly into that park. So, at about ten-thirty in the morning, I walked casually down Octavia Street and into Fort Mason Park—but I also walked into that precognitive vision I had seen as a child!

As I crossed Bay Street and entered the park, I looked to my left, and there it was. The scene I saw is the very picture that appears on the back cover flap of this book. I knew it was the exact vision because of the way the light was reflecting off the bay and the houses of the Marina on the left. Of course, the Golden Gate Bridge was right in the middle! Immediately bursting into tears, I ran up the hill overlooking the scene and let myself fully surrender to the moment—to that vision I knew I had experienced more than forty years before. I was beside myself with joy, awe, and wonder! In the midst of those profound tears of joy, I realized that I had finally found the proof for my Unified Field.

That six-year-old boy had obviously been in a state of soul consciousness, and before closing his heart, he let me know exactly where I would be when I would be seeing through his eyes again. The event I was experiencing now had obviously gone backward in time. This was my proof that there was no time and space within this state of soul consciousness and that love was indeed the sole constant of the universe! I also knew I was now ready to own this truth.

I remember taking Janet down to the park and telling her what had happened to me and telling her to never forget this brief time we shared together. I'm sure she had very little understanding of what had happened, but it didn't matter—because I did. I also remember telling everyone in advanced training that I now had the proof I needed to own my Unified Field and that owning it was now my clear intention. I am sure very few people in the class had any idea of what I was talking about and feeling, but it didn't matter—because I did.

The universe also must have known, because within six months after that event, I was propelled to a position where I had to take full responsibility for what I had discovered.

A friend of mine had sent a rough copy of my Unified Field theory to Paul Brenner, a New Age author who was on the Board of Directors of the American Holistic Medical Association (AHMA). Paul read my paper and immediately called and told me he had been profoundly moved by it. He also asked me to present it as a plenary speaker at the opening session of the AHMA annual meeting the following spring.

I spent the next six months preparing a slide presentation of my Unified Field, and in March of 1988 I presented it to about 2500 holistic practitioners in Seattle.

I'll never forget the moment I showed the last slide on the huge auditorium screen. It was a picture of me at four years old looking very wise and knowing beyond my years. (See this photo on page 103.) I told the audience that my whole journey in life had been a quest to find that child and share his great truth—a truth that each one of them also knew at the deepest level. I then pointed to the picture on the screen and told them that was who was speaking to them that evening.

I really was that child sharing his great truth— a child who had seized his moment by finally saying yes to himself.

After returning from the AHMA meeting, another incident occurred that offered further proof that this state of soul consciousness exists beyond time and space.

It was now Sunday night. I had just returned from Seattle and was sharing a tape of my talk with a group of friends. There was a great deal of mutual joy and excitement as they listened to the tape, because they all had been very supportive and encouraging during my preparation for that presentation.

However, one very important person in my life wasn't supportive. It was someone who, in the process of just being herself, had given me an important gift and was just about to give me a far more incredible gift. That person was my mother.

I had called her about a month prior to the presentation to share my joy and excitement and catch up on her activities. I felt some apprehension about the call because my mother was unfortunately an unhappy victim and martyr who had never claimed her own joy and had resented my triumphs throughout her life.

My apprehension was well-founded because the first five minutes of the phone conversation was a verbal attack in which she repeated virtually every disqualifying remark that she had ever said to me throughout my life. "You are the most arrogant, self-centered, conceited, egotistical person I have ever known," etc. etc. And then her favorite line: "It's obvious that you have a deep character flaw."

After I hung up, I was visibly shaken and tried to comprehend what had happened. But I still sent her the text of my Unified Field presentation, shared the excitement of this upcoming event, and asked her to send me one of her recent paintings.

Within a few days it became obvious why this had happened and how perfect it was! Here I was, about ready to own and share a gift I had longed to share my whole life, and what would be more appropriate than to have the one person who had disqualified my gifts throughout my life show up and totally disqualify me again. It was obviously a test. I was well beyond the point of no return, and so, in spite of my mother's reaction, I knew I had passed another test of standing alone, believing in myself, and going beyond the need for someone else's approval.

Back to the celebration the evening after my return from Seattle: After my friends left, I went to bed. Just as I was falling asleep, something very strange happened. I heard a voice calling to me, "Allen, Allen."

At first I thought it was Donna, the person I shared the house with. But then I realized it sounded like my mother.

At that point I literally saw my mother sitting on my bed. Her presence was incredibly loving toward me, which, in itself, almost fully woke me in surprise. She was trying to tell me something, but sleep was heavy on me, and I dismissed her efforts —until events brought her words to the surface of my mind three days later.

It happened when my brother called and told me that my mother had died in her sleep three days before—on the very night I had experienced her presence! I suddenly realized, after the initial shock of the news, that my mother had indeed come to me from beyond death. Not only could I feel her deep love for me, but now I remembered what she was trying to tell me: "Allen, I know. Allen, I know." Her last loving act to a child she had disqualified— but a child who had touched her heart deeply by sharing the gift of himself—was to come back to me from beyond death and let me know that she knew what I knew.

How could I not be profoundly touched by this incredible gift of love that proved to me that death is only an illusion measured by the limits of our consciousness?

All these events happened while I was still working in the nonprofit sector. But that was soon to change. Within six months of owning my

Unified Field theory at the AHMA annual meeting, it became obvious to me that it was time to go back into private practice. I felt called to prove what I deeply felt and knew.

I returned to private practice in 1989, and since then I have touched hundreds of people and helped them experience and know that they really do have a choice. I have also learned that seizing the moment is really taking total accountability for your life, saying yes to yourself, and not allowing yourself to be controlled by fear.

And now, dear reader, it is your moment!

13

connecting
with the
inner child

session four

Unless you become like little children,
You will never enter the kingdom of heaven.

—Jesus of Nazareth

In the previous session, you took total accountability for your life and for your pain. This means that
you have stopped being a victim; you are no longer
blaming anyone else for your pain or for the decisions
you have made up until now. From this place, you can
sense the potential for love in your life that you have
been denying. You've also come to understand that you
chose to be someone other than your truest self in
order to survive; but now you've made a decision to
open your heart and give the gift of who you are.

Whether you know it now or not, you are a
wonderful, loving person. You have within you all the

wisdom you need to live an inspired and joyous life. You will experience this truth directly when you come face to face with the child within yourself in Session Four—so get ready to meet the child within you!

The Inner Child Encounter Exercise

For this exercise you will need a tape recorder and your sacred journal for writing down answers. You will need some quiet music and something to play it on. The music should be soft, serene, and non-distracting. Instrumental music works well. So do recordings of ocean waves or nature sounds.

Now that you have gathered what you need, please prepare your initial space. This space is to be a conscious haven in which you can safely do the exercise. Play your music at a low volume, and stretch and move your body to loosen up physically; you need to enter a deeply relaxed state.

Then, turn on your tape recorder and slowly read the following in your most soothing voice. You may want to play the tape again after you have recorded it, so that you can play it back and do the visualization with your eyes closed. Alternatively, you can have a trusted friend read to you. Be sure to give yourself plenty of time to do each step.

Record from here:

Sit comfortably, close your eyes, and relax. Feel your body from head to toe. Take several deep breaths, and prepare to begin.

Now, I'm going to count backward from ten to one, very slowly. Completely relax with each count. Pay attention to your breathing. Focus on the physical sensations of your body, and really relax. Let's begin:

10. . . Feel your body relaxing. . . .

9. . . . Feel the breath come in and out. . . .

8. . . . Follow the music inside. . . .

7. . . . Let it take you deeper . . . and deeper. . . .

6. . . . Feel a tingling relaxation filling your body, making it heavier. . . .

5. . . . Slowly breathe in . . . slowly release the breath. . . .

4. . . . Feel how quiet your mind has become. . . .

3. . . . Slowly draw in a breath and hold it, hold it with awareness. . . .

2. . . . Slowly release the breath, and release all tension, every thought, every concern. . . .

1. . . .You are now in a deeply relaxed state. . . . Feel how peaceful it is to just sit and be with yourself. Just sit for a few moments, feeling this peace, being with yourself. . . .

You are now in a place of deep surrender, and you are open to any suggestion I give you; trust that this will lead you to a greater experience of yourself.

Now, with your eyes still closed, look around in

your inner landscape. You are sitting in the sand facing the ocean, watching the waves roll in and out. Feel the soothing warmth of the sun upon your body and your face. Smell the saltiness of the soft ocean breezes as they blow gently over your face and through your hair. Feel how peaceful it is to sit in the warm sun with the breeze blowing over you as you watch the waves roll in and out.

Now as you look to the left in this inner landscape, you notice a young, beautiful child playing happily in the surf about twenty-five yards away. The child is completely naked and tan from the sun. It appears totally at one with nature. You watch the child with a sense of delight as it walks, then runs joyfully, chasing the waves in and out, jumping, skipping, and laughing. You cannot see the child's face. But you feel the same sense of joy watching the child as this child feels playing by the sea. You watch, completely transfixed and captivated by this child playing with such innocent abandon. This child is completely unafraid, completely willing to be authentic and happy.

Now the child turns and sees you, and its face lights up with a joyful smile. It runs out of the surf dripping wet, straight toward you. Suddenly the face becomes clear. You recognize this child. This child is YOU! The child also recognizes you and runs all the way up to you, straight into your open arms. And you embrace each other. As you embrace this little child who is you and hold the child close to your heart, you feel such a deep tenderness and love.

Now the child sits in front of you, looking up intently into your eyes, with complete openness and trust. And you ask the child these questions:

. 1. "What do I need to do to completely and totally embrace you into my life?". . . Hear the answer the child provides . . . Write it down or record it.

2. "What is my deepest fear?". . . Hear the answer the child provides . . . Write it down or record it. (This child knows what your deepest fear is.)

3. "Is that fear now an illusion?". . . Hear the answer the child provides . . . Write it down or record it.

4. "Can I trust this process?". . . Hear the answer the child provides . . . Write it down or record it.

5. "What is my next step?". . . Hear the answer the child provides . . . Write it down or record it. (The child knows your next step, because that child is in a state of soul consciousness, which exists beyond time and space.)

6. Ask the child any question you would like to ask the child, about your past, your present, your future, or any area of your life . . . Hear the answer the child provides . . . Write it down or record it.

7. "Is there really joy beneath the pain?". . . Hear the answer the child provides . . . Write it down or record it.

8. "Will you forgive me for leaving you?"... Hear the answer the child provides ... Write it down or record it.

9. "How important is this work of self-healing?"... Hear the answer the child provides ... Write it down or record it.

10. "What is the single most important advice you can give me?"... Hear the answer the child provides ... Write it down or record it.

It is important now that you listen to this child very attentively and take its words very seriously.
End the recording here.

Here's some coaching to assist you in this very important visualization:

If you have done all your previous exercises and homework, you will actually meet this child within you. To the degree that you have not done all your assigned work, you may experience difficulty accessing the child. For example, if the answers you received from your child are still reflecting fear, hesitation, or reluctance to speak the truth, then you have not yet gone beyond your victim issues. This means you may need to go back and do the earlier exercises again until you have released your issues at a deeper level. This is fine. Don't rush yourself according to some imaginary time clock. You are not racing anyone. And please don't judge or pressure yourself in doing this work. You are healing yourself of lifelong patterns! So embrace and support yourself in this holy work. And be willing to do whatever it takes to heal yourself. Such an attitude is self-compassion in action.

Your recordings or written notes are very important here; this data will help you understand where you are in this transformational process. I suggest that you re-read this material periodically until you understand as completely as possible the wisdom it contains.

You may be stunned to realize that this child has been with you always, waiting inside for you to come and find it. Remember, your child is the embodiment of the soul consciousness that lives within you! This child has been guiding you to every significant relationship you've had in your life. It has been setting up the patterns in your relationships that need to be healed and resolved. This child has been guiding your quest to finally heal the original place where it was wounded; it has longed for you to do this healing work for yourself. It has also been longing for you to reach out to embrace it and to re-establish a relationship.

Your inner child is there right now to help guide you in your present healing, and in all your future choices. This child within is your best ally on your healing journey. By reconnecting to the simplicity and joy this child carries, you can heal in the present and realize that your future is a clean slate.

Your choices from now on can be aligned with your truest vision and your original state of soul consciousness. You can stop being a victim, seize the reins of your own life, and take your rightful place in this evolving and loving plan!

Homework:

Your homework has two parts:

First, spend time with this child. Become each other's best friend. Listen to and honor what this child tells you.

Listening to your child means that you are willing to follow its advice if it is given; be sensitive to the child's point of view. *Also, let this child be your teacher.* This child is connected to the joy and playful spontaneity that you once had and that you now need to tap into in order to heal and return to your original state of soul consciousness.

You have now come face-to-face with the child who truly lives within you. This child has always been there underneath your deepest pain and fears. You will feel it and know it when you fall in sync with this child who is so full of joy and aliveness. You will know this feeling as the thrill of saying "Yes!" to yourself and to living with a childlike and joyful abandon. You will feel as if a heavy cloak of doubt or sorrow or resignation has been lifted off of you. The child within you has always wanted to say "Yes!" to life. So go through your fears, say "Yes!" to the child in you, and rediscover the joy of your authentic self!

Here is the second part of your homework:

In at least six real-life situations, allow yourself to say yes to your deepest joy—regardless of the risks.

Saying yes could be as simple as saying "I love

you" to someone you have been reluctant or afraid to express this feeling to, or dancing with wild abandon regardless of who is watching, or simply giving yourself permission to do something fun or exciting that you have always wanted to do but felt self-conscious or afraid of doing.

As an example of the effect this "meeting the child" visualization has on many of my clients, I'd like to share this poem written by Howard, a man who recently flew out from New York to work with me:

Howard's Poem

Fresh and free and fantastic he did run
Into my outstretched arms
Over the crashing of the waves,
Over the loving sound of my coach's voice,
And through my tears.

His innocence glittering in the sunlight,
His eyes as bright as his smile,
Howard was finally in my grasp,
Again.

As I held him to my chest,
Our arms entangled,
Our hearts beating as one,
He let me know that this was no illusion.

He was always right here,
Just beyond my notice,
Where he continued to play,
Unfettered by all the pain and hurt,
By the raging hurricane of my life,
He remained calm.

Still playing.
Still creating.
Still laughing.
Still wondering.
Still loving.
And singing.

All while his grown-up shadow
Continued on without him,
Growing heavy and confused,
Fighting the tortured daily battles of the heart,
Oblivious,
Trying to find peace
Where none would ever come.

Through the years we climbed,
Like on a jungle gym
Set on a playground of my life.
I could barely keep up,

But his laughter always beckoned me,
Never leaving me behind.
Howard was there to smile that goofy grin,
Reminding me always
That he would be here,
As he always was.

Through the joys of my life,
He would smile.
Through the accomplishments of my life,
He would beam with pride.
Through the frightening caverns of my life,
He would hold a flashlight
And sing.

Through the deep pain of my life,
He would run his hands through my hair and
    soothe me,

Reminding me,
Like the gentle eyes of my coach,
That under the river of my life's greatest pain
Lies the joy that makes the journey a sweet one.

No more would I have to pause in panic
When some important task calls to me.
No more would I need to cry in frustration,
Wondering where my talent escaped to.

For little Howard is always there,
Keeping all that is me in safekeeping.

Holding the tools and playing with the toolbox,
Rearranging them in a thousand ways,
Just waiting to hand the right ones up to me
At precisely the right time.

Howard now knew that he truly had another choice. Guiding someone to this place of choice is all that I can do as a therapist or coach. And if you go through this self-healing process you too will arrive there. Then, like Howard, you will realize something your inner child has always known: the real coach is within you!

Three People in Search of a Choice

John's Story

John was a former professional football player who had a legion of friends but was beset with feelings of inadequacy and fears of abandonment. As such, he was continually trying to prove himself and could not truly enjoy his life and family. Not surprisingly, John also had recurring bouts with depression. These had persisted for years, and as a result, before he met me he was considering using Prozac.

John's pictures of himself as a child showed a marked change after the age of three. I therefore asked him to check with his father (his mother had passed away) to see if anything dramatic happened around that time in his life. He immediately got back to me and told me that his mother, whom he had deeply loved, had been checked into a mental institution when he was three years old. His father told John that he had become inconsolable with grief after that happened.

That was the smoking gun! Once he had finished his Life Chart, John very quickly began to realize that almost every three years he would have a bout of depression. This was particularly the case if it involved being separated from his family.

There was still a lonely and emotionally frightened child within John—a wounded and still inconsolable child that was waiting for the piano to fall on John's head every three years, just as it originally did in his childhood. No wonder John could not fully own and enjoy his success; part of him was convinced it would all end—just as his mother's presence in his life had come to a sudden end at three years old.

But when he met the child within in Session Four, John was so moved that he hugged the child to himself in total joy. His child told John to let go of his fear of being alone, that his fear was an illusion. His child also told John to stop being afraid of failure and reassured him that he would never have to suffer this depression again if he would stop being controlled by fear.

John subsequently had a complete medical checkup, which revealed no chemical imbalance. The checkup confirmed that his problem existed in his head and in the unacknowledged terror of a lonely little child within himself who was still trapped by fear. John is no longer afraid of failure or loss and can fully enjoy the abundance of his life.

Carole's Story

Carole was a workaholic who continually felt a need to prove herself. Her Life Chart and review of her early childhood revealed that her parents wanted a boy. Sadly, she had subliminally picked up their disappointment early in childhood. It was obvious to me that her continual need to prove herself was an attempt to overcome her deep feeling of unworthiness.

Her whole life changed when, while working with me, she took total accountability for her life and realized that being herself was not only enough, but that—lo and behold—she had been deeply loved for most of her life by the parents she thought were disappointed in her!

But the deepest shift in her consciousness occurred after Session Four, when Carole met the child within herself.

The child told her that her inner child was her light and joy and promised that, if she could get out of her head and into the moment, she would be seeing through the child's eyes. When she left my office after that session, she was suddenly moved to sit down on the steps for a few moments. With tears in her eyes she looked around her and realized that everything she saw was vivid primary colors. She was now literally seeing through different eyes—the eyes of the child within herself who had finally been released from a dark cocoon of fear and unworthiness.

Hank's Story

Hank was someone who, like so many of my clients, had deep feelings of childhood inadequacy and unworthiness. He had become an adult at an early age and would not allow himself to be in the moment or to fully surrender to joy and love in his relationships.

As such, he had gone through most of his life punishing the people closest to him by withholding his love. But in essence, he was really punishing himself. His current relationship was with a woman who had these same feelings of unworthiness. This time Hank could no longer run away from himself. The game was up, and he knew it.

Hank met the free and spontaneous child within himself in Session Four. And when he heard the child tell him to fully open his heart so that he could finally and truly experience himself, he literally screamed "Yes!" at the top of his lungs!

It was an event neither of us will ever forget, for in that moment he had moved beyond the point of no return. Hank reaffirmed that being himself was not only enough, it was beautiful!

Now it's time for you to say yes to yourself, to fully open your heart, and to begin to see through different eyes.

14

open your heart (there are no "but's" or "what if's" with love!)

session five

In the last chapter you contacted and got to know the child within yourself; you experienced and became more integrated with its wise, loving, spontaneous, and playful nature. Having done this, it's now time to fully open your heart. There are no more excuses!

In this session you will learn to open your heart by extending gratefulness to the people in your life, past and present. Part of this work will involve guided visualization using the same ritual space that you have set aside for previous exercises. I highly recommend that you record this guided visualization on a tape.

If possible, have soothing music or nature sounds play-ing in the background. (You can play the music in the background while you record the visualization so that it is all on one tape.) Then you can replay the tape and lead yourself in the visualization. It is important that you do this guided visualization while in a deeply relaxed state and with your eyes closed. This will allow you to totally surrender to the process and experience it more fully.

The Heart Opening Exercise

Start recording here:

Now, sit comfortably, close your eyes, and relax your body. Sweep your awareness up and down from head to toe and feel a deepening relaxation. Take several deep breaths, and sit quietly for just a moment. Now I'm going to count backwards from ten to one, very slowly. Completely relax with each count. Pay attention to your breathing. Focus on the physical sen-sations of your body, relaxing, relaxing. Let's begin.

10. . . Feel your body relaxing. . . .

9. . . . Feel the breath come in and out. . . .

8. . . . Follow the music inside. . . .

7. . . . Let it take you deeper . . . and deeper. . . .

6. . . . Feel a tingling relaxation filling your body, making it heavier. . . .

5. . . . Slowly breathe in, . . . slowly release the breath. . . .

4. . . . Feel how quiet your mind has
become. . . .

3. . . . Slowly draw in a breath and hold it,
hold it with awareness. . . .

2. . . . Slowly release the breath, and release
all tension, every thought, every
concern. . . .

1. . . . You are now in a deeply relaxed
state . . . Feel how peaceful it is to
just sit and be with yourself. Just
sit for a few moments, feeling this
peace, being with yourself. . . .

Pay close attention to your breathing. Completely
surrender and let go, knowing and trusting that this
will lead you to a greater awareness and experience of
yourself. Be aware of your feet resting flat on the floor,
connected to the earth, your deepest and most loving
support. Feel your legs . . . and completely relax. Feel
your behind, sinking into the seat . . . and completely
relax. Feel your stomach and chest . . . and completely
relax . . . Feel the gentle rise and fall as your breath
comes in and goes out. Breathe in, hold it a few seconds . . . breathe slowly out . . . and completely relax.

Now feel your hands resting on your legs and
completely relax . . . Feel your arms heavy and resting
at your sides. You are now feeling totally relaxed, aware
of how, with each breath, you sink deeper and deeper
into a place of silence, peace, openness, and trust. Feel
your shoulders, releasing all tension from them, and
completely relaxed. Feel your neck and particularly

your throat, also relaxed. Feel the air coming down through your throat into your lungs and then coming out as you exhale. Feel your head resting on your neck . . . so completely relaxed. Feel the sense of deep peace and relaxation inside your head, and feel your mind spacious and empty . . . Be here in this moment only, aware of the sound of my voice and your own deep breathing.

You are now in a place of deep openness and trust, receptive to inner guidance and help, ready to take this journey deeper into yourself. Be willing to follow this meditation wherever it leads you, knowing and trusting that it will help you in your healing process, knowing that it will give you a greater aware-ness of yourself, and knowing that it will lead you to a deeper connection with yourself and with the Unified Field of love in which you exist even now.

Now, as you look around in your inner landscape, you discover that you are in a long corridor of a very large building. You are alone, and you are safe. It is an unusual building, because there seem to be no win-dows. You are walking down the corridor. As you get about halfway, you see a door on the right-hand side. You open this door and walk into a large room. In this room is a large movie screen that reaches from floor to ceiling. In front of the screen sits a director's chair with your name on it—*(say your name here)*.

Now you sit down in the director's chair. As soon as you do, the screen lights up and the film begins to roll. The film shows a series of important figures from your adult years, that is, from age 21 until now. One by one, you see pictures of people and animals that have touched your heart from the age of 21 until now. As these people and animals appear on the screen one by one, thank them from your heart and tell them why they have been a gift in your life. For indeed each one of these people and animals has been an incredible gift on the journey of your heart. So take your time. See each one. Thank the person or animal aloud or in a whisper or within yourself—but do it with feeling. Take your time.

When the screen goes blank, sit quietly a moment, thinking about all the people and animals who have touched your heart, feeling how much they've meant to you and how much they have given to you.

Turn the tape off now, rewind to the beginning, and do the above visualization. Let it take however long it takes. When you're finished, turn the recorder back on.

Begin recording again here:
Now take a moment and consider: How many of these beings have you thanked in real life? What feelings come up in you as you consider this question? Take another moment and feel these feelings. *(Pause for 30 seconds, then continue reading.)*

The screen is now blank. You get up from your director's chair and leave the room, shutting the door behind you on the adult years of your life so far.

You continue walking down the corridor in the same direction. When you reach the end, you see a door on your left. You open this door and see a long flight of descending stairs. You go down several stories, down and down until you reach the bottom and find yourself facing another door. You open the door, go through it, and find yourself in another corridor. You turn left and walk down the corridor until you come to another door on your left. You open this door and enter another room, smaller than the last room. There is another movie screen, not quite as large as the one you were just watching, but still large. In front of the movie screen is yet another director's chair with your name on it—*(say your name).* You go and sit down in the chair. As soon as you are seated, the movie screen lights up and the film begins to run.

This film is showing you pictures of all the important people and animals who have touched your heart and contributed to you from age 11 to 20, from your adolescence to your early adulthood. As they come on the screen one by one, look at them, thank them, and let them know why they have been a gift in your life. Indeed, these people and animals have been an incredible gift on the journey of your heart. So take your time. Thank them aloud or in a whisper or within yourself, but thank them with feeling. Do this until the screen goes blank.

Turn off this tape for now and do the above visualization. When you've finished, turn the recorder back on.

Record again beginning here:

Now take a moment to consider: How many of these beings have you thanked in real life? And what feelings come up in you as you consider this question? Take another moment and feel these feelings. *(Pause for 30 seconds, then continue reading.)*

Now you get up from your chair again and go out of the room, shutting the door on your adolescent years. You continue walking down the corridor to the end, where you find a door on your left. You open this door and descend another long flight of stairs, much longer than the last. You descend for at least 10 stories.

Down and down you go until you finally reach the bottom, where you come to another door. You open this door and find yourself in another corridor. You turn left again and start walking down that corridor. Perhaps three-quarters of the way down, you come to another door on the right. You open this door and walk into another room, somewhat smaller than the last room and quite dimly lit. But you can make out another movie screen, somewhat smaller than the last screen, yet almost reaching from floor to ceiling. In front of this movie screen is another director's chair with your name on it—*(say your name)*. You walk over and sit down in the chair.

Now the movie screen lights up and a film begins to run. The film shows a series of pictures of people and animals who have touched your heart and contributed to you in some meaningful way during your early childhood years, from birth to age 10. As these people and animals come on the screen one by one, look at them, thank them, and let them know why they have been a gift in your life. Indeed, these people and animals have been an incredible gift on the journey of your heart. Take your time. Thank them aloud or in a whisper or within yourself, but thank them with feeling. Do this until the screen goes blank.

Turn off this tape for now and do the above visualization. When you've finished, turn the tape back on.

Begin recording again here:

Now take a moment to consider: How many of these beings have you thanked in real life? What new feelings come up in you as you consider this question? Take another moment and feel these feelings. *(Pause for 30 seconds, then continue reading.)*

You have now thanked all the people and animals you can recall in your life who have touched your heart and contributed to you in some meaningful way. But it is important to realize that there are probably many more of them who have touched your heart and contributed to your life that you simply cannot recall. We are all surrounded by more love than we tend to realize or remember. So, take a moment to feel all the love you've been surrounded by throughout your life.

Ask yourself how much of this love you noticed at the time. Right now, do you feel and fully receive all this love that you were given from your birth up to the present? Feel your heart open to receive it. Feel it fill your heart, even your physical body. How does it feel?

Take a few moments to drink it in. The love of all of these people and animals in your life has always been there, waiting for you to receive it. You have carried this love inside you your whole life without knowing that you did. And it will always be there. So sit for the next few moments and simply feel it.

And realize this: If you've been punishing people by withholding love from them your whole life, you now know, sadly, that the person you have punished the worst is yourself. *(Pause 30 seconds, then continue reading.)*

As you continue to sit and watch the screen, a new set of pictures begins to appear. You see your first childhood home. But now, instead of simply watching from your chair, see yourself actually rise from your chair, walk into the screen, and enter the house through the front door. Now you, as the adult you are, go exploring the house of your childhood, looking for your parents, your siblings, and whoever else lived with you or was important to you . . . perhaps even your grandparents. You are going to find them all, one by one, and speak with them. But first you must find yourself as the little child who lived in that house. You are now going to talk to this child who is you.

Now you approach an open door and see yourself playing alone on the floor in your old room. The child who is you looks up into your eyes, knows exactly who you are, and accepts this in a natural way.

Now you sit down on the floor next to the child, and looking into its eyes, you say, *"(Your name),* you no longer have to be afraid of not being loved for who you are. You no longer have to try to be someone else to be worthy of love. You no longer have to be afraid that being yourself is not enough. You no longer have to be afraid that those whom you love deeply are going to leave you, abandon you, or stop loving you. You don't have to be afraid any more about anything. I am your friend and your true self and I will always be with you and protect you and love you and take care of you. I am now willing to feel all the pain and sadness and fear that you have carried for so long inside me. Because underneath it all is an eternal reservoir of joy and peace and love. Everything in my life has lead me here, to you, and I cannot go any further on my life path without you, without the purity, innocence, and joy that you carry. Are you ready to go with me?"

Now listen closely to the child's answer.

If the child says no, then ask the child why it is afraid of going with you and assure it that it is now safe and you will never leave it again. If this happens, and you make a heartfelt appeal to this child who is you, it should respond with a yes the second time you ask it to come with you. If the child still hesitates, you may still be carrying victim and resentment issues from the past and have not taken full accountability for the feelings that you felt and the decisions that you alone made. In that case, you must fully review Session Three.

If the child says yes, which happens almost 100 percent of the time, you are ready to say good-bye to your relatives. Now you take the child by the hand and go to the living room. There you find your father sitting on a couch. He looks up and sees you, recognizes you, and accepts your presence there in a natural way. Looking into your father's eyes, still holding the child's hand, you say, if it feels appropriate, "Father, thank you for giving me the gift of life. Thank you for being there for me, for loving me and taking care of me as best as you could, and for allowing me to love you—as best as I could."

Tell your father whatever feels right for you. If other words feel more appropriate, say them now. Perhaps you need to forgive him for not being emotionally available to you—or for even more serious abuses of his parental role. The important thing is to complete (open your heart) with your father with as much feeling and love or compassion as you can, avoiding the victim role and releasing any negative charge or emotion you may still carry toward him. You may ask him to forgive you for shutting down, for checking out, for holding resentments toward him, or for any other offense you feel you may have committed toward him. Realize that by speaking to your father in this way, with full, free, and honest expression, you are giving him the gift of your authentic self, the deepest part of who you really are. And realize that this is the greatest gift you have to give. Now, from a place of compassionate understanding, love, forgiveness, gratitude, and joy, say good-bye to your father.

Now go and find your mother. Perhaps she is sitting at the kitchen table, or in a chair where she often sat. She looks up and recognizes you and accepts your presence there in a natural way. Now, looking into her eyes, thank her for giving you the gift of life. Thank her for being there for you, for loving you and taking care of you as best she could, and for allowing you to love her as deeply as you could have. If other words feel appropriate, speak them instead. Tell her whatever feels right for you. Perhaps you need to forgive her for not being emotionally available to you or for other failings or even abuses of her parental role. The important thing is to complete with your mother with as much feeling and love or compassion as you can, avoiding the victim role and releasing any negative charge or emotion you may still carry toward her. You may ask her to forgive you for shutting down, for checking out, for holding resentments toward her, or for any other offense you feel you may have committed toward her. Realize that by speaking to your mother in this way, with full, free, and honest expression, you are giving her the gift of your authentic self, the deepest part of who you really are. And realize that this is the greatest gift you have to give. Now, from a place of compassionate understanding, love, forgiveness, gratitude, and joy, say good-bye to your mother.

Next, still holding the child who is you by the hand, find and thank your siblings, if it feels appropriate. Looking into their eyes, thank them one at a time for being your brother or sister and for sharing the adventure and the ordeal of your childhood with you. Tell them that you forgive them, or ask them to forgive you, for any grudges, conflicts, incidents, or unresolved issues that may have burdened your relationship. Tell them that you did not know how to express these feelings to them when you were children, because of your deep sadness and aloneness, which they also carried. Realize that by speaking to your siblings in this way, with full, free, and honest expression, you are giving them the gift of your authentic self, the deepest part of who you really are. And realize that this is the greatest gift you have to give. Take a few moments to do this now. *(Pause now for one minute, then continue reading.)* Now, from a place of compassionate understanding, love, forgiveness, gratitude, and joy, say good-bye to each of your siblings.

Now, as you have done with your parents and your siblings, also do this with any of your grandparents with whom you had a significant connection, whether or not they actually lived in this house with you and whether or not they are still alive. Also do this work of completion with any other significant people in your childhood who may have raised or helped to raise you. All the while you are holding the hand of the child who is you.

Now, having interacted with all these important people from your childhood from a place of understanding, compassion, and love, you and the child leave the house together, shutting the last door on your childhood, closing it gently but firmly behind you. Now the two of you begin walking together down the street, away from your childhood home. Soon the house is far behind you and you come to a curve in the road.

As you come around the curve, you will see someone standing there, waiting for you. That person may not appear right away but be patient . . . That person *will* appear. When the person appears, look closely and see who he or she is. Whoever the person is will be totally appropriate, for this person represents something about the stage of the journey of healing that you are now on. Look closely and take your time until you see this person clearly.

Once you recognize this person, relax deeply, concentrate on the sound of your own breath, and come back to the room in which you are sitting. Now count slowly from one to ten, bringing yourself back to an alert yet still deeply peaceful awareness. When you are ready, open your eyes.

End recording here. Rewind the tape and do the above visualization.

Now here's some special coaching for completing this session:

First of all, ask yourself: *Who was the person waiting for you around the corner?* If it was you, this means that you have established a very deep connection to your authentic self at this stage of your journey. If it was a parent, grandparent or other loved one you were deeply connected with as a young child, this tells you that you are getting closer to that child within yourself. If the person waiting around the corner is someone you know from after childhood, such as a lover or mate, consider what that person represents to you or means to you, what role that person has played in your life, and what he or she has contributed to your journey. Ponder these things until you have a sense of the meaning of this person's appearance in your vision, both in relation to your childhood and in relation to your current adult life.

The person waiting around the corner may be a religious or spiritual figure or archetype or some other well-known figure. Whatever or whoever this person is will be important, so try to interpret the significance of this person's appearance in relation to your original childhood life experience or your present adult life experience.

Thanking and completing with the significant people in your life can be very powerful. And don't worry if during this exercise issues came up for you with certain individuals. This is normal. Be willing to set aside further time to work on these issues, both inside yourself (as you've just done here) and directly with these people, if it is possible and appropriate. Of course, the more complete you are with the significant people in your life, the more you will benefit. (We will continue to work with these key people in the home-work assignment that's just now coming up.)

This guided visualization also lets you see that despite the self-protective cocoon you had created—and regardless of how shut off you may have felt from others—there have always been people who have loved you and contributed to your life. It is very important for you to thank them.

Even those who have passed on are still with you on your journey through life, spiritually present in your heart, in your psyche, perhaps even in the room with you as you do such exercises as these; they too need to be thanked. (You may have felt their presence while doing this exercise. Please don't discount any such feelings or perceptions; they are real. My own grandfather recently appeared to me in a dream, bearing an important message that helped me make a very difficult personal decision.)

In closing, let me summarize: To fully own your power and give the gift of yourself on this planet, you must really thank the people who have shared your journey and who have played a significant role in it, as you will also do in your homework. And when you can accomplish this completion from a place of deep understanding, love, forgiveness, compassion, gratitude, and joy, you will find more freedom within that will allow you to share yourself more fully wherever you go. This is what I mean by "singing your song."

There isn't one person in my life who has deeply touched my heart that I have not thanked. It's a great way to live. Remember, "God only reveals Himself to a grateful heart."

Homework:

Your homework is to actually thank those people in your life to whom you have not yet expressed thanks, and to do this in person.

With each person you thank, you will be completing something, leaving the confines of your cocoon, and sharing the gift of yourself with the world. Remember, the aim is to speak to these people from a very deep place. So if you need more preparation for this event with certain people, "rehearse" for it internally as you've done in the exercises above. Rehearsing will allow you to continue releasing and resolving these issues within yourself until you really feel you can speak to these people authentically, with conviction, and in person.

If you engage these sessions with deep intention, your heart will begin to expand and open wider and wider. This may bring you tears of joy. For in the last phase of this seven-session process, the phase I call the Fires of Attrition, the final remnants of unworthiness and resentment (and you will feel unworthy to the degree that you still harbor resentments) are burned away by tears of joy as you realize how deeply you are being loved and have always been loved. Only your self-imposed, self-protective cocoon has kept you from experiencing and living from that love and, worst of all, acknowledging that love. Remember, the worst prison is a closed heart!

Also please remember this: We are doing action-oriented work. Illumination comes only after transformation. Transformation comes only after *action*. There is no change without action. Action changes knowledge into wisdom. and action always involves risk.

So if you want dramatic results, you must do these exercises and this homework with passion. Once you do them, you will be beyond the point of no return. Having tasted freedom and experienced your true self outside the cocoon, you will never want to go back inside again, no matter how safe it seems. This is how you will fulfill the promise of healing yourself, which I proclaim in the subtitle of this book.

Again, the ultimate YES to yourself is to fully express love and open your heart, and the greatest remorse and ultimate NO to yourself is not to express that love. So open your heart and hop on the Real You Express. It's your turn!

Tom's Story

Learning to Accept Love

Tom was a reluctant believer in this process until he got to Session Five. He was a successful group facilitator in a company that teaches self-awareness seminars throughout the Pacific Rim countries, and therefore he believed he understood himself. But Tom had work to do: He was in reality a professional caretaker—a role he had learned early in life—and he had never taken his turn.

This man was very effective at what he did, but it was virtually impossible for him to accept being loved. He had deep feelings of unworthiness that began in early childhood and had never dealt with them. Now these feelings were affecting his relationship with his family. And because he was in service from a place of unworthiness, he was rapidly "burning out." He was referred by a friend who had worked with me and had experienced the process.

When Tom got to Session Five, he finally realized he had been loved by scores of people but had never been able to fully accept their love and had thanked virtually none of them.

For Tom, the "person around the corner" in the exercise you just completed turned out to be a childhood friend whose name was Hector. But when Tom came out of the visualization, he laughed and said this was ridiculous because Hector and he had not really been that close and he saw no need to contact him.

I told him to call Hector anyway. There had to be some important reason for Hector being around the corner. "Just do it!" is one of my favorite expressions.

So Tom reluctantly called Hector and, by virtue of following my lead, walked into the most traumatic painful event of his childhood! He was not consciously aware of this trauma, but the child within himself had never forgotten. After Tom nervously introduced himself, after all these years, Hector related an amazing story to Tom. Hector recalled that Tom had become deeply attached to Hector's family during his early childhood years. He was especially attached to Hector's older brother Paul. Tom's relationship with Paul had in fact gone so well that Hector had been jealous of their deep connection. (It was here that Tom began to feel butterflies in his stomach.) Hector then dropped this bombshell: "Don't you remember how devastated you were when Paul was tragically killed in an automobile accident? We never saw you after that, even though you were like family."

That was enough! Tom burst into tears, the tears he had stuffed when the older brother he had always wanted (Paul) was taken away from him. These healing tears eventually led him to the sad little boy within himself who had closed his heart. This boy was convinced that other people's happiness was more important than his own. "I don't deserve to be loved," he had told himself. "People I love deeply will leave me." In our work together, we saw that this conclusion was rooted in the deep trauma of his loss, the loss of his best friend, Paul.

It did not take long for Tom to fully open his heart and claim the love and joy that was deepest within himself. And it also did not take long for Tom to begin to trust the unknown parts of himself and the child within, who had led him to me, to his friend Hector, and to another choice in his life.

So now, are *you* ready to accept love and create another choice in your life?

15

the death exercise and the life review

session six

*In the evening of this life,
it is on love we shall be judged.*
—St. John of the Cross

The following set of exercises is one of my most powerful creations. In it you will come face-to-face with every fear you are still holding onto and taste a form of freedom you have yet to access. You will also find out, in this chapter, whether you have really made a difference on the planet—and in the lives of all of the people you love.

Today you are going to die.

This session involves a two-part exercise: the Death Exercise and a Life Review.

To start, you will need to prepare your ritual space with a very specific prop. This prop, a simulated body in a coma, will be the focus of the first part of the exercise. You have two options to create this prop: (1) You can have someone you trust and feel connected with consent to lie under a sheet up to the neck on a bed or a couch. (2) Or you can arrange pillows, blankets, stuffed animals, or any other objects you feel close to on a bed or couch to represent a body, then cover it with a sheet, leaving the "head" visible.

The Death Exercise

Having done your preparation, sit down at the side of the couch. But note: In this exercise, the person lying beside you in a coma is *you!*

Usually in my sessions with my clients, I play the part of the person in a coma. And I tell them to imagine the following scenario:

Imagine that you are driving home from work or the store and your car is struck in a head-on collision by a black semitrailer. Your injuries are massive. You are extracted from your mangled vehicle and rushed to the hospital, where you lie in a coma for two days. The five people you most cherish in this world are there in the hospital, praying for your recovery.

The doctor in charge of the intensive care unit comes to these five people and tells them that your condition is suddenly and rapidly deteriorating and

that you probably will be gone within the hour. He
then tells your loved ones that there is a special way to
commune with patients while they are in a coma. You
can do this, he says, by sitting with them, holding their
hand, establishing emotional/spiritual contact, and
then asking questions—to which the comatose person
responds by squeezing your hand.

Now, imagine again that you are the comatose
person. The doctor tells your group that he has been
relating with you in this very way, and that you have
told him, through your hands, that you are about to
pass on and wish to commune with your loved ones
one last time before you go. The doctor then allows
each person to go in to your bedside and say good-bye
to you. (For this exercise, I suggest you have some
Kleenex handy!)

In the Death Exercise, you will play the role of
each of the five people who comes to complete with
you prior to your death. You will take a minute or two
to feel your connection with this person, and to project yourself into that person's psyche and see yourself
through that person's eyes, thoughts, feelings, and
memories. You will speak to your dying self, who will
be lying on the couch, from the point of view of each
of the key people in your life. Try your best to do this
as if both of you were truly in this situation.
Remember, each person is very close to you, has come
to say a final good-bye to *you*, and time is very short.
For each person, use the format below. Be sure to cover
each of these five points for each person who comes to

complete with you as you lie on your deathbed.

- "(Say your name), this is (say that person's name), your (mother, father, child, sibling, friend, lover, etc.) Can you hear me?"

- Express how it makes you (as each person) feel, that you are dying.

- Express gratitude and acknowledgment for the gifts *you* gave them in your life. Be specific. Really consider, from this person's point of view, how you may have contributed to this person and enriched his or her life.

- Express whether or not you (as each person) feel you really knew the dying *you*. And express how you (each person) feel about that.

- (As each person) express your love for the dying *you*.

Now, stop reading, prepare yourself and the ritual space, and do this entire exercise with each of the five people saying good-bye to you. Do not continue to read until you have done this. When you have finished, engage the inquiry below, and then go straight to the Life Review.

Having done the exercise above—having viewed yourself from within the psyches and feelings of these significant people in your life—take a few moments to consider the following questions:

- Did these people really know you?

– Just how well did they know you?

– What parts of yourself can you now see that you withheld from them?

– Did you push any of these people away because of illusionary fears?

– Did you push these people away because of fears of nonacceptance, lack of self-worth, or the belief that being you was not enough?

– Did you push them away, or hide yourself from them, for any reason at all?

Be honest! Take a moment and write down in your journal (under each person's name) any insights that have come to you along these or any other lines.

During this first part of the Death Exercise, most clients discover that only one or two of those closest to them know who they really are. They also find that they have, to a large extent, kept themselves hidden from most of the significant people in their lives.

The Life Review

The following background will help you prepare for the next part of this session, which is your Life Review.

As has been documented by Elisabeth Kubler-Ross, Raymond Moody, and other researchers, the near-death experience—which I elaborated on in Chapter 6—begins with a Life Review in which the near-death experiencers who have "gone into the light" are able to then review their own lives and literally assess the success or failure of their life mission. In essence, we "judge" ourselves, although this judgment is based on compassionate understanding, not righteous anger. It appears, by all reports, that when we die, we will judge ourselves according to the life we have lived, by how fully or well we played our part, by how fully we loved or allowed ourselves to be loved, by how much we were controlled by fear, and by how much we gave of ourselves or how much we withheld ourselves from others. And we will judge ourselves in order to come to a deeper understanding of ourselves and the purpose of our lives, not as a means of punishment for our failings and mistakes.

These studies support the concept of God as a loving plan in action, rather than a God of vengeance and judgment. In fact, I know of no near-death reports so far that describe an experience of harsh judgment meted out by some patriarchal (or even matriarchal) deity. So chances are it probably won't happen to you either.

Keeping this cosmic data in mind, it's now time for a dry run of your own death.

I want you to lie down and pretend that you are dying. (If it helps, you can pull the sheet over your head, but it isn't mandatory.) Imagine that you are still lying in the hospital, eyes closed, in a coma. The last person has completed with you and said good-bye. Your life on earth is finished. You deeply relax, release, and let go of your body; your life functions come to rest, and you die.

You now enter the afterlife, and begin to experience a full Life Review, as this is what will initially
happen when you pass away. Imagine yourself leaving
your body and rising up to look down at yourself as
you review your life. Ponder deeply the following
questions:

  — "Did I allow myself to love others as fully
    and completely as I could have?"

  — "Did I really let others in?"

  — "Did I fully allow myself to be loved?
    Or did I run away from love?"

  — "Did I really let others know who I am?"

  — "Did I really know who I am?"

  — "Did I make any difference on this
    planet?"

  — "What more could I have done to make
    a greater difference or contribution?"

  — "Did I resolve lingering resentments?"

  — "Did I clear up problems with
    those important to me?"

  — "Did I really become an authentic
    person?"

  — "How well did I understand myself?"

  — "Did I thank others for the gifts they
    gave me by their love and friendship?"

  — "To what degree did I allow myself to
    be controlled by fear?"

  — "Did I do everything in my life that
    I truly wanted to do?"

- "Did I make of my life all that I truly wanted to make of it?"
- "Did I really live my dreams?"
- "Did I fully open my heart?"

While you are still pondering these questions and answers (and writing your answers in your sacred journal), record the next visualization, with soothing background music or nature sounds. Then play the tape and lead yourself through the visualization.

The recording begins here:

Now you find yourself passing rapidly through a dark tunnel. You hear ethereal music and find yourself in a beautiful meadow surrounded by trees, flowers, and butterflies. You now are experiencing the most awesome, exquisite, profound state of consciousness . . . It is truly sublime. And so familiar . . . Of course! You are experiencing your original state of soul consciousness. There is no sense of separation from anyone or anything. You are connected to all, to everything.

You lie in this meadow in this profound state, drinking it all in. Now you see people who have passed on before you also there with you. People whom you loved. They are also enjoying the same state of soul consciousness, so joyous and peaceful, and are as happy to see you as you are to see them. One by one, they come to you to touch you, stroke your hair, look at you lovingly, lighting up with smiles of joy at seeing you again.

Suddenly, far off, you see a person bathed in light coming toward you. As the person draws near, you now realize that it is you, uncloaked from fear and radiating light. This radiant being greets you, and then speaks to you and says, "*(Your name)*, why didn't you let your light shine fully while you were on the planet? What were your reasons for hiding your light, for holding back? Tell me, what were you afraid of?"

Now list for yourself all the "reasons why" you have not fully opened your heart and let your light shine in your life. Feel the pain and the cost of this withholding of yourself from those you love, the cost of withholding the gift of yourself from life. Realize that you still have time to change this. Decide that you're going to go back and make up for this "lost time," that you're going to complete this unfinished business by opening your heart to your loved ones and sharing yourself fully with them. Make a list of all the things you're going to do when you go back. The essential promise you must keep to yourself is to fully open your heart and to let your light shine with each person in your life, regardless of the risks.

Your days of punishing people or protecting yourself by withholding love and yourself from them and from life are over. See that you have in reality been punishing yourself, even as you tried to protect yourself in this way.

Now, rewind the tape and play back this important visualization.

Now that you know how many (or how few) of the people in your life really know you and you clearly see your unfinished business, it's time for one more exercise.

This time imagine that the five people who visited you on your deathbed are now on *their* deathbeds. You must complete with each of them and say goodbye. One by one, tell them the following:

- What it means to you that they are dying.

- How you feel about their dying.

- What gift or gifts they have given you.

- Whether you feel you really know them or not, and how it feels either way.

An important note here: The degree to which you fear to speak honestly to these people about these things is the degree to which you haven't really known them and also the degree to which you've hidden your true self from them and never let them in far enough to see your heart.

I'm sure that you have many "good excuses" for this withholding, for why you haven't fully expressed and revealed your true self to these important people in your life and for why you've settled for not really knowing who they are. But all these excuses are your recipe for living a mediocre life—a life, I might add, that will not make for the most scintillating, satisfying Life Review. So why not change this sad state of affairs while you still have time? Why not live a life you'll look forward to reviewing after all is said and done?

To begin this new life, you must complete your old life by opening your heart to your closest loved ones, by sharing your deepest feelings with them, fully and honestly, regardless of the risks. You must share yourself with them in person (or by phone if they live far away), regardless of your fears that tell you to keep hiding yourself and your deepest feelings from others until the day you die. (How many years and how many lifetimes have you done that already?) You must do it! You owe it to yourself! Pick one person, and begin this process!

"But they'll think I'm weird! They won't understand! It'll be awkward!" I can hear you protesting already. That is your fear speaking, and it keeps you from opening your heart to the people who matter to you the most. But when you come from love, the deepest part of them will feel, understand, and receive your honest and heartfelt communication with the most profound gratitude. I've had clients who shared themselves fully with their parents only to have their parents want to become part of the process and come to a session! Doing these exercises is not about changing or even helping these people in your life (although it may do just that!). It is about *you healing yourself* by finally expressing who you really are to others! It is about giving the gift of yourself to life!

Here's some extra coaching for doing this session: Most people find out through this exercise the degree to which they have withheld the full expression of their true self from the people who are closest to them. And they realize that they still have more homework to do with these key people. It is very sobering to be confronted with this profound withholding of our true self from the people who matter the most to us. It is even more sobering to contemplate just how we would feel if these people died before we had a chance to *really* know them or to finally share ourselves with them and allow them to know us.

Despite your fears about fully sharing and expressing your deepest self and feelings, there is something you must understand: When you are ready and willing to make this shift, regardless of the risks, those to whom you most need to express yourself will know it on a deep subconscious level. When you take action and finally move beyond your fears to connect authentically with others, a deeper part of them is actually waiting and ready for this to happen. Opening your heart and going beyond your fear in this way proves, with certainty, that you can be your authentic self and participate fully in life from now on!

Homework:

Your homework is to share yourself, in the way described in this chapter, with the important people in your life.

Please note: You must do the exercise *without* saying it's a Death Exercise. Create an occasion in which you open your heart with each one of these people. Let them know, one by one, what a great gift they are, as if they, or you, were going to die tomorrow! Start opening your heart with the people closest to you. Watch what happens.

There is not one person in my life that I love, or have loved, who does not know why I love or loved them. I have expressed to all of them what incredible, wonderful gifts they are to me. Should they or I die tomorrow, we will have known each other for who we really are. No unfinished business or complicated debris. *What a great way to live!*

Remember, the greatest remorse is love unexpressed. *Never hold back your love. And never hold back from love.* Love is the full and honest expression of your true self and your deepest feelings. When you withhold love, you lose touch with others and with who you really are. Withholding love and the full expression of your authentic self is the ultimate NO to yourself! What a huge opportunity to miss! So, say YES to yourself and do your homework now! Let those you love know how deeply you love them, why you love them, and why they have been gifts in your life. Do this exercise and feel your heart expand in the process.

Remember, in the world of ego consciousness, the greatest risk and fear is being your true self. But that risk and fear is an illusion! In the realm of soul consciousness, taking the risk of being your true self not only liberates you from fear but also connects you to the Unified Field of love, your ultimate source of joy.

Risk –Author Unknown

(Edited by Allen Roland)

To laugh is to risk appearing the fool.
To weep is to risk appearing sentimental.
To reach out for another is to risk involvement.
To expose feelings is to risk exposing your true self.
To place your ideas and dreams before a crowd is to
    risk their loss.
To love is to risk not being loved in return.
To live is to risk dying.
To hope is to risk despair.
To try is to risk failure.
But risks must be taken, because the greatest hazard
    in life is to risk nothing.
People who risk nothing, also do nothing, have
    nothing, and are nothing.
They may avoid suffering and sorrow, but they can
    not learn, feel, change, grow, love, or live.
Chained by their certitudes, they are slaves who have
    forfeited their freedom.
Only a person who risks is free.
And the greatest risk
Is to fully open your heart and truly share and
    be yourself!

Tony's Story

Learning to Share the Deepest Feelings

Tony was a man who had been leading a life that was filled with possessions, but in constant denial of his deepest feelings. He had a very successful business, which he had inherited, and spent most of his time dreaming up ways to spend his money. Every month he seemed to be buying a new car, a new boat, or new golf clubs in a frantic attempt to avoid feelings and emotional attachment. His relationship with his wife was very shaky, and not surprisingly, he was in the midst of an affair with someone who was as emotionally unattached as he was. When he came to me, he was getting bored with buying so-called happiness and decided to take a peek inside himself just in case there might be something wrong.

Remember, I do not put Band-Aids on egos, so very quickly Tony realized that there was indeed something wrong: He had left behind, early in his childhood, a little boy who was convinced that no one would see or hear him if he really shared his deepest feelings.

Tony would leave two-hour sessions with me totally exhausted. But every time, he found himself strangely excited as each layer of his false persona was revealed for him to examine and deal with. At the same time, I would continually remind him that beneath that ego shell was a real and joyful little boy who has always wanted to feel and love deeply. When we did the Death Exercise which you have just completed, he was devastated. He realized that no one in his life really knew him, and he had pushed away most of the people who wanted to know and love him, including his own parents and wife. The only one he hadn't pushed away was his dog Mickey—and only because this was undoubtedly a safe relationship!

I knew his wife was on the verge of leaving him, and I told him that sooner or later he would suffer a loss that would finally force him to deal with the well of grief that he had been running away from his whole life.

However, he was still bargaining with his expensive toys and wasn't about to go inside, even though he had by now, in working with me, reached a place of choice.

Then it happened. He called me a few days after our last session, literally beside himself with grief. He wanted to see me right away, which I arranged for that afternoon. He burst into my office, crying openly, and exclaimed that his dog had died, that he had done everything possible to save him, but that it didn't work. He was inconsolable—he was in the well of grief! He said, "I'll do anything to get him back, Allen, anything—please help me!" I told him that the only way he could connect again with his dog was to fully share the feelings he was sharing with me with his wife and to fully open his heart with her, as he had with Mickey.

"Just do it!" I said, and he knew he now had no other choice. Happily, Tony was able to carry out this important sharing with his wife. In the process, he finally opened his heart, claimed himself, and saved his marriage. Tony and his wife now have three beautiful children, and the first was born a year after the death of Mickey. They named their firstborn son Michael in honor of Mickey. Mickey lives!

Now the question becomes—are you ready to fully open your heart like Tony and really live?

16

many are called, few listen, still fewer respond

session seven

Be kind, for everyone you meet is fighting a hard battle.

— Plato

If you have come this far, you now know that to feel greater joy, you must be willing to feel any fears, pain, and difficult feelings that stand in the way.

You also understand that in this life, no one remains unscathed; we all check out to avoid the same unbearable pain, and we are all on our own quest to heal our primal wounds and rediscover the truths we all knew as children.

Furthermore, you've also realized by now that the people who have been in your life have behaved as they did on account of things that happened to *them*— because of the choices they then made and who *they* became as a result! These people did the very best that they could, given the circumstances and the level of consciousness they had acheived.

And you've therefore understood that who your mother and father were (and are)—and how well they have loved you—was predicated on who *their* mothers and fathers were and how well their *own* parents had loved them.

And finally, it should be clear to you by now that *nothing was ever personal. Nothing that happened was ever about you. All were acting from their own unhealed past.* The wounding from which every ego is born has been passed down for so long that its origins will never be traced—but you can now break that chain!

And now that you've done as much of this work as you have, it is my hope that you've decided, irrevocably, to become your true, authentic self—and to share the gift that you are with life, regardless of the risks or the consequences.

Remember, love is at the root of every decision you made. Who you are *is* love. And the more you stop hiding yourself from the people with whom you've felt so much love and so much pain, the sooner will you disembark from the Ego Local and board the Real You Express.

All aboard! It is now time for Session Seven, my

favorite session, which is all about inner listening and guidance.

There are two types of listening that are the basis of this chapter:

Ego-based listening is what we do when we are controlled by fear and running away from love—and away from ourselves in the process.

Soul-based listening is what we do when we are consciously going through fear and running toward love—and ourselves in the process.

Before we begin the exercise for Session Seven, there are seven key insights to bear in mind in preparing for soul-based listening:

1. *We are always being called to the path of the heart.*

Like a great magnet, soul consciousness continually pulls at us, imploring us to surrender to love and become one with source, one with the Unified Field of love. Why? So that we can fulfill our own, unique function within a rapidly evolving and loving plan.

And how does the soul call us? Through dreams, synchronistic events, relationships—and even, at times, an audible call.

For example, I have dreamed precognitively about every major relationship I have had, ever since I made my transition from the outer journey to the inner journey. Each of these relationships led me to open my heart more fully—and, in the process, to claim and experience more of my authentic self.

2. The soul contains the events that shall befall it. And you can sense these events if you internally listen with your heart.

Words cannot convey the incredible joy of knowing that your life is being divinely guided from within by the Unified Field of love, and that the events that cross your path are an ordained part of your destiny.

The more you *listen to* and trust your own internal guidance, and the more you respond to it with an open heart, the greater that joy becomes and the more you realize that being you is not only enough—it's beautiful!

3. Most people do not listen to these inner calls from the soul, simply because they are afraid of losing control.

The ego is all about fear, control, and protection. It is so very comforting for me to know that there are many things happening in my life that I have no control over but that nonetheless enhance my life and my work. I enjoy knowing that my life is being divinely guided, as is everyone else's. The next story you read, after this session, is a perfect example of listening and responding to the inner call in this way.

4. Love cannot be controlled; if it finds you, love will direct you!

In his book *The Prophet*, Kahlil Gibran celebrated this compelling power of love when he wrote:

When love beckons to you, follow him,
Though his ways are hard and steep.

And when he speaks to you believe in him,
Though his voice may shatter your dreams

As the north wind lays waste the garden.

For even as love crowns you so shall he
    crucify you.

Even as he is for your growth so is he
    for your pruning.

All these things shall love do unto you
    that you may know the secrets of your heart,
    and in that knowledge become a fragment
    of life's heart.

And think not that you can direct the course
    of love, for love, if it finds you worthy, directs
    your course.

Our ultimate calling is to surrender to love and let
it direct our course, as Gibran declares. In responding
to this inner call, we fully embrace ourselves and our
destiny. Indeed, we cannot escape our destiny, and it is
divine!

5. So few listen, and still fewer respond, because
so few trust the unknown or the love and joy
that is deepest within themselves.

The human ego wants nothing to do with the
unknown—for the unknown, in actuality, refers to the
mysteries of our soul and the love and joy within. And
ego death is the eventual result of deeply listening to
and responding to our soul and entering into the
Unified Field of love.

6. Being in love ultimately means being in service—which means being you!

What is the biggest gift—the greatest service—you can give somebody else?

If you say "unconditional love"—you are only partially right.

If you say "taking care of the person"—you are missing the mark.

If you say "myself"—you are totally right! The biggest gift you can give anyone is the gift of *yourself.*

Yes, *you* are the gift!

What does that mean? It means singing your own, unique song and owning your love and joy in a world of victims. It means being authentic and real in an unauthentic and artificial world. It means being willing to stand alone and yet know that you belong!

If you have the courage to do this, you will experience the ultimate joy of being part of something far greater than yourself and knowing that you are being used in a universal loving plan.

7. We are all emissaries of love on a mission to a planet whose inhabitants are in the process of making a shift in consciousness.

As such, our common purpose is to open our hearts and remove the cloak of ego consciousness so that we can let our light shine, sing our song, and become part of the same loving plan. This is our common quest. Bearing these insights in mind, let's now turn to our last exercise.

As with the previous exercises, I recommend that you record this guided visualization on a cassette tape, with soothing background music or nature sounds if possible, but this isn't necessary. Now, the exercise:

Record from here:
You are now ready and sitting comfortably in the space you've set aside to do this work. Close your eyes, relax your body, and take several deep breaths. Now begin to count down slowly from ten to one while concentrating on your breathing and the deepening relaxation of your body. With each count, feel every part of your body relaxing and opening in total peace and trust. By the time you reach "one," you will be in a place of deep receptivity, completely open to this guided journey, knowing and trusting that it will lead you to a greater awareness and experience of yourself. Now let's begin the count.

10. . . Feel your body relaxing. . . .

9. . . . Feel the breath come in and out. . . .

8. . . . Follow the music, inside. . . .

7. . . . Let it take you deeper . . . and deeper. . . .

6. . . . Feel a tingling relaxation filling your body, making it heavier. . . .

5. . . . Slowly breathe in, . . . slowly release the breath. . . .

4. . . . Feel how quiet your mind has become. . . .

3. . . . Slowly draw in a breath and hold it, hold it with awareness. . . .

2. . . . Slowly release the breath, and release all tension, every thought, every concern. . . .

1. . . .You are now in a deeply relaxed state . . . Feel how peaceful it is to just sit and be with yourself. Just sit for a few moments, feeling this peace, being with yourself. . . .

Pay attention to your breathing and completely surrender to this experience, knowing and trusting that it will lead you to greater awareness and experience of yourself. Be aware of your feet flat on the floor, connected to the earth, your deepest and most loving support. Feel your legs, completely relaxed. Feel your behind sinking into the seat, completely relaxed. Feel your stomach and chest, the gentle rise and fall as your breath comes in and goes out. Breathe in, hold it a few seconds. . . . Breathe slowly out.

Now feel your hands resting on your legs, totally relaxed. . . . Feel your arms relaxed and resting at your sides. You are feeling totally relaxed. Notice how, with each breath, you sink deeper and deeper into a place of peace, openness, and trust. Feel your shoulders, all tension released from them, completely relaxed. Feel your neck and particularly your throat, completely relaxed. Feel the air coming down through your throat, into your lungs, and then coming out as you exhale. Feel your head resting on your neck, also completely relaxed. Feel the sense of deep peace and relaxation inside your head, your mind spacious and empty. . . . Be here in this moment only, aware of the sound of my voice and your own deep breathing.

You are now in a place of deep openness and trust, receptive to inner guidance and help, ready to take this journey deeper into yourself. Be willing to follow this meditation wherever it leads you, knowing and trusting that it will help you in your healing process, knowing that it will give you a greater awareness of yourself, knowing that it will lead you to a deeper connection with yourself and with the Unified Field of love in which you exist even now.

Now, as you look around in your inner landscape, you find yourself leaning against a giant oak tree and looking out over an incredibly beautiful meadow of green grass, full of flowers, and surrounded by birch trees. Everything is alive with color, the blue of the sky above you, the green grass that surrounds you, the white of the birch trees, the beautiful flowers—orange, yellow, red, white—and the colorful butterflies. A doe and two fawns are grazing in the meadow not too far away. And you can hear the melodious babble of a nearby brook. As you look up into the blue sky, you see an eagle soaring above you on a wind current. What an extraordinarily beautiful vision it all is, nature simply present and alive as herself.

And now, leaning against this oak tree, taking this all in, you realize how blessed and embraced and loved you are by nature. This very oak tree is even now breathing in the very carbon dioxide you are exhaling and breathing out the very oxygen that you are even now inhaling. What more intimate connection could there be than this life-giving exchange of breath? And this intimate exchange of energy between you and nature and all other living beings is going on unceasingly in innumerable ways, and has been going on night and day since the very dawn of creation. You are connected to the birch trees, the dancing flowers, the vibrant green grass, and the atmosphere, which extends to the heavens above and which is composed of all of these elemental energies. Even the flowers and butterflies seem to be telling you that joy is always here to be grasped and opened to in each fleeting moment. The brook is telling you that life always flows ceaselessly and joyously and that you can surrender to and become a part of that flow. The eagle soaring on the wind is telling you, "You too can fly!"

And you can do all these things if you will just open your heart and give full expression to who you really are. Then you will be playing your part in this loving plan with all of these wonderful creatures and all of nature. Now take a moment to feel how deeply loved and nurtured you are by nature. Nature is always embracing you, calling you to sing your song and to join in the great harmony of the loving plan—just like the oak and birch trees rustling in the breezes, like the babbling brook, the soaring eagle, and the wind itself.

Now, put your hands over your heart, breathe in, and acknowledge with a deep feeling of gratitude the truth that you are always being loved by nature with the most profound and unimaginable intimacy that is possible. Acknowledge that nature is always calling you to respond with the playful spontaneity of a child, to sing your song and play your part in this magnificent loving plan. As you breathe in this feeling awareness, look into the surrounding meadow.

Slowly, people are emerging from the edges of the birch trees, walking into the meadow, coming toward you. You recognize every one of them. These are the people who have loved you the most in this life, who have seen and embraced your uniqueness, your beauty, your spirit. All the people who have played a significant role in your life and that you wish to be here right now have come to greet you, to touch or embrace you, to stand beside you, to acknowledge you in whatever manner feels appropriate to you.

You know who these people are. They may be your parents, siblings, relatives, lovers and friends past and present, your wonderful children—all those whom you've loved and who have loved you, who have recognized your unique nature and seen your heart. They have all come out into the meadow to gather around you and to be with you.

One of the last to come into the meadow is the little child within you who has patiently longed and waited so many years for your final recognition and embrace. This child, now an integral part of your being, leaps into your lap and joyfully embraces you.

Now in the distance you see another figure, bathed in light. As this figure draws closer, you realize that it is your soul-conscious self. You greet your brilliant and illumined self, the source of so much healing wisdom, with a smile of gratitude and love. Now your Light self hands you a gift wrapped in silver foil and takes a place among your other beloved companions on your journey. All watch as you slowly open this gift, unwrapping the silver foil—to find a beautiful mirror inside.

You lift up the mirror, look into it deeply, and into the eyes of a person who is not afraid to love or laugh —a person who is not afraid to be honest, is not afraid to sing his or her song, and is not afraid to be his or her true self. And suddenly you realize...*You! You are the gift!* Just as everyone there has been a gift to you. *You* are the gift you've always wanted more than anything. *You are a gift to life*, like the oak tree behind you and the birch trees surrounding you, like the flowers and butterflies adorning the meadow, like the eagle soaring on the wind, like the blue sky and the babbling brook—if you will simply sing your song, as nature does.

Let the words *"I am the gift"* resonate in your soul. You are a gift to life whenever you show up in life just as you are, as your authentic self. When you express your deepest feelings and open your heart to those you meet, you will enrich their lives. Likewise, they will enrich your life by being who they are, if you will open your heart to receive them. Decide here and now that you will no longer withhold the gift that you are from life. *Be the gift.* Let this truth be alive in your open and loving heart and present in your very soul.

Now, take a few natural breaths with feeling and awareness. Slowly open your eyes. Remember what you saw when you looked into the mirror. Remember how you felt in the meadow, surrounded by all the people you've loved. Remember your child within leaping into your lap and giving you a loving embrace. That child is still within you as a source of joy, love, and guidance. All you have to do is listen and respond. All you have to do now is come out of your cocoon and fly—by continuing to let others into your heart and into your life, and by sharing the gift of your true self with others, regardless of the risks.

You stand on the threshold of an inner freedom that you have longed for your entire life. The freedom to be who you really are is the greatest joy in life. So listen to the guidance that comes from within. Trust and respond to it by showing up as who you truly are. Surrender to that which is far greater than you, to the source of your very being. Surrender to the Unified Field of love. There is no greater joy than this.

The Listening Story

Meeting My Mentor by Following Inner Guidance

Let me give you a personal example of how our lives are always divinely guided from within if we will but listen and respond.

In 1972, I attended a three-day conference for graduate students in counseling at a place called Westerbeke Ranch, in Sonoma, California. By this time it was nearly a year since I had surrendered to the "well of grief" in my relationship with Karen and my whole life had shifted from being outer-directed to inner-directed. I had also experienced a profound dream during this inner transformation that pointed to my writing a book entitled *Conscious Love, the Ultimate Energy*.

At the time, I was also making a transition from the brokerage business to the counseling profession and was enrolled at Sonoma State University in a master's degree program.

Many paranormal events happened to me during this inner transformation. These occurrences led me to seek out the renowned parapsychologist Stanley Krippner to be my mentor for my master's thesis. Luckily, it turned out that he was leading the conference for master's degree students I was about to attend.

At the opening session, Stanley asked a group of about twenty students what their thesis topics would be. When he turned to me, I somewhat nervously announced that I was going to write a book entitled *Conscious Love, the Ultimate Energy*. There was some laughter around the room. Stanley then pointed to me and said, "Demonstrate it," which produced even more laughter.

The conference ended a few days later. Much to my chagrin, I had not made a meaningful contact with Stanley, who had already left and would be flying to New York City the following day.

While carrying my bags to my car as I was preparing to leave the ranch, something within me told me not to leave. So, I put my bags down and wandered over to the dining room, completely surrendering to whatever was guiding me.

No one was in the dining room, so I peeked into the kitchen and noticed that someone was washing dishes. He seemed to be part of the cleanup crew and immediately recognized me as one of the participants in the conference. He asked me if I would have a glass of wine with him and chat for a few minutes.

We sat down in the dining room where he proceeded to share his perceptions of the conference. This man was of the belief that the whole conference had revolved around him.

I listened compassionately and nonjudgmentally and then gently, but directly, helped him to see another, more realistic perception of what had happened. We then finished our wine, he thanked me, and I now knew I could leave the ranch. I had no idea what this was all about, but I had completely surrendered to it and had simply shown up with this man.

Later that evening, Stanley Krippner called me at home and told me that he was for unrelated reasons canceling his trip to New York the next day and wanted to meet with me in Sausalito. Stanley and I spent the next afternoon together. He told me that when his chauffeur had come back from the ranch the previous evening after working with the kitchen crew, he seemed like a changed person—he had made a dramatic shift in behavior and attitude. When Stanley asked him what had happened, he said that he had had an extremely illuminating conversation with me and was now seeing things quite differently.

Stanley suddenly realized that I had indeed demonstrated that conscious love was the ultimate energy by facilitating a complete change in the behavior of his chauffeur; because of this, Stanley now knew we had work to do together. He thereupon became the supervisor and mentor for my master's thesis and was responsible for connecting me with Grace Petitclerc, who became a key guide on my path toward fully owning and sharing my truth. But Stan also became my second reader for my doctoral dissertation and has been an ongoing source of support and guidance.

This story is about the power of showing up and sharing our truth—even at the risk of being laughed at, which I was.

This story is about listening and responding to an inner guidance—which, in my case, said, "Get out of the way, Allen. I'll take care of this."

This story is also about the power and magic of surrender and letting go of control.

Now the question for you is: Do *you* have the courage to listen, respond, and surrender to your inner guidance?

17

relationships are the proving ground for who we really are

> *The only right love is that between couples whose passion leads them both, one through the other, to a higher possession of their being. . . . Union, the true upward union in the spirit, ends by establishing the elements it dominates in their own perfection.*
>
> —Teilhard de Chardin

Can you imagine what relationships would be like if they were founded in the recognition of a Unified Field of love? On the truth that each of us has an authentic vocation within an evolving and loving plan? Such relationships would be seen, not as ends in themselves, but as means to an end. That end would be the fullest flowering of both partners' unique gifts and the deepest realization of their soul-conscious connection to the Unified Field.

Such is the true purpose and context of all our significant relationships. When we do the steps outlined in this book and find our true self, we also discover that every significant person in our life was a profound gift—regardless of the outcome of the relationship! We come to know that even those relationships in which we experienced the deepest terror and pain were leading us to the deeper joy and purpose that lay beneath. Rediscovering ourselves through the vehicle of relationships is our prime directive and our greatest test. This singular task is the work we are meant to do together in our most intimate relationships.

In this chapter, we are going to gather the key arguments of this book and apply them to relationships. In my nearly three decades of work with couples, I have found that there are at least seven key insights that seem to apply universally to the path of loving, committed relationships.

1. Conscious love serves the highest interests of both partners regardless of the risks to the relationship.

Most partners see the purpose of a relationship as the mere fulfillment of their emotional and physical needs; this is what I have called emotional or conditional love. But the conscious love motive goes much further: It also seeks and serves the full flowering of our partner *regardless of the consequences or risk to the relationship.* This lofty goal is not easy for couples. Conscious loving requires the courage to let go of the ego's need to stay in control, to possess, and to avoid pain. But for those who pass this threshold—for love is indeed the threshold to another state of consciousness—the payoff in spiritual growth is immense.

2. Relationships are the proving ground for who we are (as the title of this chapter declares).

Stop for a moment and ask yourself: How far have you gone on your own Cycle of Life? For example, are you still facing issues of unworthiness? Do you harbor fears of abandonment? Have you fully opened your heart? Look to your most intimate relationships. Their status in this regard—more than anything else—is always the truest indicator of who and where you are in your own personal growth.

The singular reason for this truth is that, for both partners, unresolved issues with parental figures will always come to the surface during the relationship. Remember, this is why your inner child leads you to every partner in the first place. It wants you to finally recognize, confront, and resolve the original wounds that caused you to separate from your true self and retreat into your cocoon of ego consciousness. These unresolved issues of betrayal, abuse, rejection, or abandonment must be re-enacted, because emotionally that is where we are still stuck.

*3. The ego always externalizes the inner quest
and always projects its primary wounding scenario
onto the present circumstance or relationship.*

You cannot heal these wounds and fulfill your inner quest until you stop looking outside—toward a partner or circumstance—for an answer that can be found only within. This misguided search of the ego explains the astounding divorce rate in the United States and the conventional holding patterns in which most relationships eventually become mired. There is no use journeying to the mountain when the mountain is within you.

4. Authentic relationship begins when both partners realize that their quest will be fulfilled not in any "perfect relationship," but only when they reunite with their authentic self, which is still trapped within a prison of childhood fears.

This means that the state of one's relationship with one's self sets the stage for every love relationship. And every intimate relationship re-creates that childhood prison for both partners—until they finally choose to "escape" by opening their heart and surrendering to love *in the face of their fear and pain.*

As I have explained, until I understood these things, I repeatedly "fell into" painful relationships with beautiful, emotionally unavailable women like my mother. Then in 1972, I was finally able, with Karen, to re-experience the full depths of despair and aloneness

I had felt with my mother when I first decided that "being myself is not enough." Only when I totally surrendered to, and took full accountability for that deep repressed pain, without emotionally checking out and denying love, did I realize that no partner was the "answer." The real answer was to recognize, embrace, love, and heal the pain of the sad little boy within me —the little boy who always wanted to love that deeply and who had finally emerged from hiding. Virtually all my clients enact versions of this experience, repeating their own wounding childhood scenarios. There is no question in my mind that what all of us are looking for, in our intimate relationships, is—our self!

5. In our most intimate relationships we are always looking for permission to truly be ourselves and to finally be loved for who we are.

A key question to continually ask ourselves in relationship is, "Am I truly being myself, or am I compromising myself and my values for the sake of the relationship?"

Milton Avery has written, "To be able to be oneself and not have to disown one's values to please another—that's what intimate love is all about."[1] In other words, intimacy ("into-me-see") is authentic only to the degree that it is based on our being who we truly are with one another. And we do this by fully and honestly expressing our deepest feelings and self with one another *regardless of the risks.*

Important note: This injunction is not a license for unleashing our harsh emotional baggage on one an-other. *Such abusive behavior is the unconscious reenactment of the wounding scenario.* Our truest self and our deepest feelings must come from a place of love and soul-conscious compassion, not from victim-based ego consciousness. Expressing ourselves from this place requires an open heart that inevitably brings us closer to our partner, even when communication is necessarily of a difficult nature.

6. We love ourselves only in the same measure that we can honestly express ourselves and be ourselves within an intimate relationship.

This is a corollary to the fifth insight above. However much our egos may fear honesty and intimacy, this is really what most of us long for instinctively. For example, I usually ask couples in counseling, "What do you really want from your partner?" Very often their answer is "honesty" and "deeper intimacy." (Not surprisingly, either is not really possible without the other!) In these sessions, couples will often say things like "Please be honest, even if you think it will hurt me." In other words, we all crave honesty because it is the doorway to intimacy.

7. Love is not about control; love is about surrender!

There is no painless path to soul consciousness; we are all being drawn to that path like moths surrendering to a flame. Much to the ego's chagrin, this path is not through the mind; the true path is surrendering through the heart. So what exactly does surrender mean? It means letting go of the ego's need to control and defend. It means being totally present with an open heart to whatever we feel in the moment. It means opening to love in the presence of our own fear and pain. It means being seemingly *out of control.*

As we've seen, surrendering to love is much like our original birth passage, for we are surrendering to a force far greater than ourselves. As such, love represents another profound passage—in this case through the "birth canal" that leads from ego consciousness to soul consciousness. Obviously, the experience of love is a dire threat to the ego, for it represents the kind of raw, heartfelt feelings and emotional vulnerability that the ego was created to avoid at all costs. These are the difficult feelings that initially drove us into our cocoon in the first place! Indeed, love is not an easy path—but love is the only path that can lead us through our deep unworthiness issues and the illusionary fear that "being myself is not enough."

Having looked at these seven key insights of relationship, let us now consider what I believe to be the three basic types of relationships we tend to set up in our quest to find ourselves. These three types follow logically from the seven principles above. They are as follows:

1. "Going-through-the-motions" relationships

Here both partners are joined by common fears and are usually completely dependent on each other. Little, if any, passion exists, few risks are taken—and no significant growth occurs. This type of relationship is primarily motivated by the most basic needs, such as survival, security, and the avoidance of loneliness and fear. Both partners have settled for less than all of themselves, but at the cost of passion and growth.

Going-through-the-motions relationships are like a dry creek bed waiting for the spring rain.

Color it gray.

2. "Safe Love" relationships

Here the ego still dominates the hearts of both partners, who share common disaffinities—lack of self-worth, fear of love and intimacy, and so on. This kind of relationship is usually intense and short-lived. Each partner vainly tries to fill the other's emotional void (Mission Impossible) and vainly expects the other partner to fill his or her emotional void (Mission Impossible II). In the end, Safe Love is a lose-lose relationship. Any relationship that is externally directed is little more than an ego cocoon built for two. The love between the partners tends to contract rather than expand. Still, even a Safe Love relationship is a step in the right direction. Personal growth can occur here, although it is a bit like driving with one's foot on the brake rather than on the accelerator.

Eventually, if the partners don't move beyond the Safe Love mode, the relationship can easily become destructive. Because of the lack of real fulfillment or healing, the partners will begin to take out their deep inner resentments on each other, acting out their primal wounding scenarios with no effort to resolve them. At that point, both partners become "wound-mates" and the relationship will either end, usually dramatically, or deteriorate into a Going-through-the-motions relationship.

The only way this relationship can grow is to take the path described in this book: Both partners must go inside, choose to release the ego's need for control, surrender to the heart's need for love, and support each other as true partners in this process.

In a Safe Love, the dry creek bed has now become a stream.

Color it pastel.

3. "Soul Mate" or "Great Love" relationships

Soul mates come into our life when we are ready to find and fulfill our part in the loving plan. Such Great Love relationships are internally directed; they prepare us for the transition from ego consciousness to soul consciousness. The ultimate aim of such a relationship is for both partners to fully emerge from their cocoons of fear and become their truest self. This is the love whose passion, as Teilhard de Chardin writes, leads the couple "one through the other, to a higher possession of their being."

As we've seen, a Great Love relationship does not serve the ego's need to control and defend its own interests. Great Love confronts us with our deepest feelings and fears—and demands that we surrender! It requires us to grow beyond our fear to the place where we can both consciously and unconditionally love our partner. It is a love that can both take hold and let go, for it is beyond emotional dependency.

There is tremendous happiness in soul mate relationships because there is no greater joy than going (and growing) through our fears and discovering our true self. This love is not for the faint of heart; indeed, many who briefly experience this fire will quickly run for cover. But they are actually running away from themselves.

You are now in the river of life.

Color it vibrant primary colors.

It is worth emphasizing that true growth in relationship comes not only from taking hold of love but, just as important, letting go with love. In that regard, my own growth has greatly been accelerated by my willingness to let go in relationship and literally feel my heart and myself expand into the light of soul consciousness. A wonderful example of that is the story I already shared of how I let go of my relationship with Rachel and, in the process, claimed my original joy, intention, and purpose. It is very important to note here that I let go of the relationship, but not the love that I felt. This practice allowed my heart and myself to expand and grow.

Maya Angelou poignantly expresses this point in her poem "Recovery":

> A last love,
> Proper in conclusion,
> Should snip the wings
> forbidding further flight.
> But I now,
> reft of that confusion,
> am lifted up
> and speeding toward the light.[2]
>
> —Maya Angelou

The great French novelist, Stendhal, a noted chronicler of human drama, chronicled six stages of love.[3] These are listed below together with their meanings, which I've added.

Stage 1. Admiration—*"I really admire you."*

Stage 2. Beginning of desire—*"I want to get to know you better."*

Stage 3. Hope—*"I hope you feel the same way."*

Stage 4. Inception of love—*"I think I'm falling in love."*

Stage 5. First crystallization [we see the beauty and perfection of the other person]—*"I'm in love and you're perfect."*

Stage 6. Doubt and/or jealousy and fear [I would also include mutual anger and resentment]— *"You're not perfect and you're going to reject or abandon me."*

This is as far as Stendhal got, and interestingly enough, it's about as far as most relationships go.

As a therapist, I believe that Stendhal is right in that most, if not all, relationships arrive—or end up at—his Stage 6. In this stage we normally withdraw from relationship, physically or emotionally, since the object of our love is seemingly causing us unremitting pain.

To resolve this crisis, we must go inside and see how we are re-enacting with our partner the primal wounding scenario from our early childhood. Remember, we are performing this re-enactment for the hidden purpose of finally healing this wound and reconnecting with our true self. As such, we must be willing to take total accountability for our personal choices and our emotional pain—while in the relationship—and restrain from any need to blame our partner. If we can do this, while not denying our love, we may reach what I believe is a seventh and final stage:

Stage 7. Roland's second crystallization—we feel through our pain to the love, beauty, and perfection within ourselves. *"It's more important that I love me than that you love me."*

Stage 7 is a relationship lived in the rarified realm of shared soul consciousness. All key relationships are a potential means to that blessed end. To reach Stage 7, we must be willing to take hold and to let go; we must be able both to cleave to and to completely give up the one we love. To reach this apex of loving, we must be willing to dwell in this paradoxical place. And only conscious love—the highest form of love—has the power to do both.

Again, to let go of the person we love *does not mean to stop loving that person*. (That approach, in fact, is how emotional love avoids the "trial by fire" required to become conscious love at Stage 7.) Letting go means keeping our heart open as we release the fear, pain, dependency, and self-doubt that might cause us to cling desperately to our partner.

Most couples come to me in Stage 6 having reached an impasse. I always tell them in our initial visit that I have no investment in their staying together. But I make one thing clear: The more they are willing to support each other's individual quest to rediscover and live as their true self, the more likely they will reach a deeper level of intimacy, trust, and commitment. How far they go along that path is up to them. It is an on-going choice for love.

They always respond positively to this approach because their search for their self is the reason they entered into the relationship in the first place (and came to me in the second place)—whether or not they were consciously aware of their motives! Of course, the most difficult work occurs outside my office in the crucible of their relationship.

Let us restate and summarize: Our quest to heal our childhood wounds and become our true self unfailingly eventually leads us to someone who shares or mirrors our own fears and issues surrounding intimacy, self-worth, trust, and love. We seem to require an intimate other on whom to project these primal scenarios and fears, and who will also reflect them back to us. This projection/reflection allows us to see what is otherwise hidden within ourselves. Then, even as we feel the pain of the original wound, we can finally choose to take responsibility and heal ourselves. *We do this by keeping our heart open and choosing to love in the place where we originally emotionally checked out, shut down, and closed our heart.*

This taking of responsibility never happens at the same time for both partners. One partner will always go first and thereby risk the relationship. As such, this letting-go process can happen within the relationship and with the same degree of pain and aloneness as an actual separation.

Jerry Jampolsky writes, "Love is making friends with fear because fear is the constant companion of intimacy."[4] But if instead we allow ourselves to be *controlled* by this ever-present fear, it will eventually override love as well as our deepest joy. To reach Stage 7, we must completely open our heart in relationship even as we come face-to-face with our deepest fears of intimacy, loss, and abandonment. The only way out of fear is to surrender through it while still choosing to love. Doing so will turn all our fears into speed bumps on our path to wholeness, freedom, and joy.

Thus, by fully opening our heart to another beyond our fear and pain, we literally embrace and own our deepest self. This is how relationship becomes the proving ground for who we really are. Yet even this is no guarantee that the relationship will survive in its present form. In Stage 7, it becomes clear that living as our true self is more important than the survival of a relationship with someone else!

What in the end happens if we reach this place of choice and actually *choose* to be authentically who we are? The message of this book is that we will have thereby healed the original childhood wound that we inflicted on ourselves, back when we abandoned our true self in exchange for the conditional love of others. Only when we reach this stage can we truly give each other the ultimate gift, the gift of who we really are.

A true Stage 7 relationship is a dance of intimacy. In this dance, both partners support and unconditionally love one another. Both share their deepest selves regardless of the risks to the relationship. Together they grow in inner joy, inner validation, courage, and freedom as they take their place in the divine and loving plan whose foundation is the Unified Field of love.

Only poetry can do justice to the music and power of this love, so allow me to share with you my own poem on the power of love.

> I want to write about the power of love—
> How it asks me to surrender,
> How it won't accept NO,
> How it laughs at my fears,
> How it shatters my expectations,
> How it grinds me to nakedness,
> How it kneads me until I become pliant,
> How it forces me to listen,
> How it demands that I respond,
> How it fills me with wonder,
> How it christens me with faith,
> How it awards me with understanding,
> How it anoints me with compassion,
> And finally, how it reveals
> The greatest gift of all—
> My self.

There are many paths to the river, but the last step is always surrender. Only by fully surrendering to love, and defeating fear, can we take the final step and swim in that deep-running river of soul consciousness—the mother and source of us all!

18

the truth that shall set everything ablaze

No problem can be solved from the same consciousness that created it.

—Albert Einstein

Most of the problems that we create for ourselves arise from our separateness from one another—from the fear of love that is the basis of what I have called ego consciousness. And therefore I must ask: Is not a radical shift to connectedness and soul consciousness *the solution* to the myriad of problems we all face on this planet?

The purpose of this book has been to accelerate this planetary shift into unity by offering you the seven self-healing sessions that comprise radical therapy.

My purpose has also been to give you an understanding of the Unified Field of love, to bring you to that place of choice where you can fully open your heart—and, above all, to lead you to take responsibility for the love and joy that is deepest within you.

What I believe you will see—if you have done the work of the seven sessions—is not only a loving plan beneath the surface turmoil of this planet but, more important, your unique and thrilling part in this plan. And I hope to enlist you in this loving plan. For I foresee that your greatest joy, as mine is, will be knowing that you are part of something far greater than yourself and to realize that you have a vitally important part to play in it.

Performing your role in the loving plan means that you must express and reveal the beauty of your authentic self, as I have with you. If you can do this, I believe you will see—as I have—that the deep underlying unity of the universe is indeed a psychic energy field of love and soul consciousness—and that the entire universe is one elemental field of *love*. The recognition of this Unified Field of love imparts a profound simplicity to the surface complexity of our lives. And in the end, this realization places a responsibility upon each of us—*to simply love one another.*

If more of us accepted and lived according to the principles of a Unified Field of love, much, very much, would change:

*We would look upon our children as the true
blessings that they are.*

We would see them as miraculous repositories of
soul consciousness, as precious little ones who have
been put in our hands for tender care and guidance.
Our educational system would be geared toward nurturing the flower of that soul consciousness as well as
recognizing the uniqueness that each child brings to
this planet as its potential contribution to the divine,
loving plan.

*Our elderly would not be looked upon with
disdain or pity.*

—but would be treasured and honored for their
long life experience, hard-won wisdom, and soul-
conscious gifts.

*Marriage and relationship would not be
viewed merely as a theater for playing out the
drama of meeting our routine emotional needs.*

Rather, our unions would be viewed as sacred
vehicles for fulfilling our deepest needs to heal, to
grow, and to play our unique part in the loving plan.

*Understanding our true life purpose, we would
each strive to experience the profound joy of soul
consciousness.*

We would aim to become capable of unconditionally loving others, and of realizing our innate connection with the Unified Field of love.

But can it really be this simple?

Yes it is. For when the truth of a Unified Field of love is realized collectively, simple solutions will spring forth from our hearts that will resolve the complex dilemmas that were originally created by ego-based thinking. I cannot state it enough: The solution to all dilemmas is ultimately love—that is, our return to soul consciousness in which the separated ego, and all ego-based conflicts, can be transcended and resolved.

Teilhard de Chardin implied the reality of such a Unified Field when he posited the existence of a universal soul that united and joined the universe and all humanity through love. In his last unpublished work, Teilhard wrote of the inevitable consequences that will arise when this truth appears:

> Sooner or later there will be a chain reaction . . . for the truth has to appear only once, in one single mind, for it to be impossible for anything ever to prevent it from spreading universally and setting everything ablaze.[1]

And the fiery truth is that the original joy within us is *God*—for God *is* love. Love itself is the ultimate life force; love alone lies as the foundation of a vast evolutionary process. Each of us participates in this joyous evolution as cocreators who are willing to go out and set *everything* ablaze by opening our hearts and sharing our gifts.

If this great arc of evolution, individual or collective, is to fulfill its destiny, we must therefore choose to surrender to love regardless of the risks—and thereby find the inspiration to love others. By doing this, we will each in the end find our path to healing and to our deepest self.

Jesus, Buddha, and all the great spiritual figures were in this sense divinely human. They were evolutionary forerunners of a state of soul consciousness that we can and must attain in order to evolve. The humanizing of these archetypal spiritual figures is an essential step that will lead each of us to do as they did: take total responsibility for manifesting the very same love and soul consciousness that always exists within each of us.

When we choose to love beyond our fear, regardless of the risks, and to fulfill our deepest propensity to unite with one another, we also fulfill the promises of attainment and redemption that Jesus and the other great spiritual figures represent.

Stephen Mitchell said it well in his *Gospel According to Jesus:*

> What is the gospel according to Jesus? Simply this: that the love we all long for in our innermost heart is already present, beyond longing. . . . The ultimate reality, the luminous, compassionate intelligence of the universe, is not somewhere else, in some heaven light-years away. It didn't manifest itself any more fully to Abraham or Moses than to us, nor will it be any more present to some messiah at the far end of time. It is always right here, right now.[2]

Those of you who are awaiting Christ's return, look within, for it is there that he resides. He resides in our deepest propensity to unite with and love one another. Or, as Stephen Mitchell goes on to say:

> The messianic dream of the future may be humanity's sweetest dream. But it is a dream nevertheless, as long as we don't transform ourselves. And Jesus, like the Buddha, was a man who had awakened from all dreams.[3]

Thus, we must awaken from all dreams that require looking for an answer "out there." We must finally go inside, face our deepest fears, and claim the only true answer: ourselves.

As I've stressed throughout this book, the path of transformation is not easy; there are no shortcuts to soul consciousness. Further, this path is not through the mind but through the heart—even through what has been called the "heart of darkness" in each of us. Teilhard called this difficult process of transcending the ego and ego consciousness the "crisis of conversion." We must each feel our way through this darkness until, through conversion, we reach the blazing light within.

How comforting it is amidst this painful transformation to realize that deepest within us is joy, intention, and purpose as well as our original loving state of soul consciousness—the Unified Field of love.

It really is this simple!

Which brings us back to ourselves and how we relate to each other in light of this truth of a Unified Field of love. To repeat a key theme of this book: We engage the Field particularly in the realm of feelings. For you must remember: Love is the ultimate sensory experience or feeling. More than a century ago, John Ruskin wrote: "The ennobling difference between one man and another is that one feels more than another."[4] It is indeed our willingness to feel, and to share from the heart, that breaks down our self-imposed walls and allows the beauty within each of us to be seen. These heartfelt sentiments break through the physical and psychological barriers that separate us from each other. We do not truly communicate with anyone until we commune with that person through feelings. There is a profound difference between deeply communing with others and merely communicating information to others. Relationship is indeed the testing or proving ground for learning to commune our deepest feelings and, in the end, for establishing ourselves in our human perfection.

When we surrender to the universal love that is deepest within us and take full responsibility for this love in our actions with one another and the planet, we will realize that we have never been alone in the universe. And if we all do this, we will experience, planetwide, that Unified Field of love.

When the heart achieves its desire, you shall transcend time and space.[5]

These words by Mahfouz—the great Egyptian poet who won the Nobel Prize for poetry—state a profound truth that this book has been aiming to demonstrate. For the heart's desire is to fully love and sing its own authentic song, thereby transporting it beyond all known limits. I knew this at four years old when, filled with joy and love, I leaned out that window in Newtonville, Massachusetts, and realized that I was not alone. I profoundly felt my deep connection with the beauty of nature all around me. I felt my oneness with all, for I had, indeed, transcended time and space, and I was in a blissful state of soul consciousness. My heart's desire has always been to feel and love that deeply again. To feel once more my oneness with all. To see through those same eyes that had transcended time and space, and to share the truth of what I see from a place of gratitude and service—as I am now sharing with you.

Only by fully surrendering to love did I find this holy grail—as you will, too!

And, in the end, this is our common journey: to reunite with the state of soul consciousness that we all once knew as children:

- a state of consciousness that binds the universe with its universal urge to unite
- a state of consciousness that lies beyond ego consciousness
- a state of consciousness that lies beyond death
- a state of consciousness that lies beneath our deepest fears
- a state of consciousness that can be truly experienced only by surrendering to love

But can it really be this simple?

Yes, it is!—and, this is the truth that shall set everything ablaze!

The twelve major truths this book reveals

1. You can heal yourself by surrendering to love. It is really that simple!

2. The long sought for Unified Field is a psychic energy field of love and soul consciousness—which lies not only beyond time and space but also beneath our deepest fears.

3. The so-called laws of science and physics are essentially observer-dependent—in that the consciousness of the observer determines what can be truly seen.

4. This Unified Field of love and soul consciousness is the absolute constant of the universe—in that, within it, time and space do not exist.

5. The near-death experience is, in reality, a state of soul consciousness that lies beyond our present state of ego consciousness.

6. Our life is a clearly defined quest, not a struggle, to emerge from our present state of ego consciousness and reunite with our authentic self and our original state of soul consciousness.

7. Beneath our deepest pain and grief is a state of love, joy, and soul consciousness the Unified Field of love.

8. Jesus was divinely human—an evolutionary forerunner for a state of soul consciousness we will all surrender to eventually.

9. There is no such thing as an ugly soul; we all come from a place of love, joy and soul consciousness.

10. Relationship is the true test of who we really are—and every love relationship, regardless of the pain, is a gift on the journey to find and embrace our authentic self and our authentic vocation in the loving plan.

11. Most long-term therapy is thinly disguised codependency; we all have the capacity to heal ourselves if we will say yes to ourselves and not be controlled by fear.

12. Darwin had it wrong—evolution is fueled by social cooperation and altruism. We cannot escape our destiny and it is divine!

For more information about Allen Roland's work or to contact him directly:

http://www.allenroland.com
allenroland@earthlink.net

Notes to the chapters

Chapter 2

1. Steven Hawking, *Black Holes and Baby Universes* (New York: Bantam Books, 1993), 99.
2. Lincoln Barnett, *The Universe and Dr. Einstein* (New York: Bantam Books, 1957), 112-13.
3. Pierre Teilhard de Chardin, *The Phenomenon of Man* (New York: Harper and Row, 1967), 265.
4. Ibid., 63.

Chapter 5

1. Lincoln Barnett, *The Universe and Dr. Einstein* (New York: Bantam Books, 1957), 34.
2. Ibid., 36.
3. Ibid., 36.
4. Ibid., 109.
5. Eric A. Cornell and Carl E. Wieman, "The Bose-Einstein Condensate," *Scientific American* (March 1998), 40.
6. Lincoln Barnett, *The Universe and Dr. Einstein* (New York: Bantam Books, 1957), 114–17.
7. Pierre Teilhard de Chardin, *Human Energy* (New York: Harcourt, Brace and Jovanovich, 1962), 72.
8. Bernard Towers, *Teilhard de Chardin* (Virginia: John Knox Press, 1966), 32.
9. Pierre Teilhard de Chardin, *The Phenomenon of Man,* (New York: Harper and Row, 1967), 264.

10. Lennart Nilsson, "The First Days of Creation." *Life Magazine* (August 1990).

11. William Emerson, "Infant and Childbirth Refacilitations." (Paper presented at a meeting of Pre- and Perinatal Psychology Assoc. of North America, San Diego, CA, 1985).

12. Carl Jung, *Memories, Dreams and Reflections* (New York: Vintage Books, 1963), 325.

13. June Singer, *Religion and the Collective Unconscious* (Chicago: Zygon Religious Press, 1969), 318.

Chapter 6

1. Teilhard de Chardin, *Activation of Human Energy* (New York: Harvest, 1970), 404.

2. Elisabeth Kubler-Ross, "Interview with Elisabeth Kubler-Ross." *People Magazine* (November 24, 1975).

3. Andrew M. Greeley, "The Impossible, It's Happening," *Noetic Sciences Review* (Spring 1987), 7.

4. As far back as 1975, in a *New York Times Magazine* article entitled "Are We a Nation of Mystics?" (January 25, 1975), Andrew M. Greeley and William C. McCready reported that almost four out of every ten Americans have felt the experience of a powerful spiritual force. Their article cited a national survey in which the participants who had felt this force were asked to check off suitable descriptions of the experience. Virtually 50 percent of the answers fell within these six:

> 1) A conviction that love is at the center of everything.

2) A feeling of deep and profound peace.

3) A sense of joy and laughter.

4) A feeling of being beyond time and space.

5) A certainty that all things would work out for the good.

6) A sense of one's own need to contribute to others.

These are all aspects of the state of soul consciousness. Other elements reported in the study that were characteristic of this state of consciousness were:

1) The interviewees perceived the phenomenon as fundamentally cognitive—not a person or a vision necessarily, but the way things really are.

2) The core of the event was a transcendent knowing. Joy, peace, light, and other aspects of the experience were perceived as the results of this knowing.

3) There was a curious loss of time perspective associated with the ecstatic interlude. "Time stood still" was a phrase they heard frequently. It was during that period of time confusion, apparently, that the unity and convergence of all things were perceived.

5. Raymond Moody, *Life After Life* (New York: Bantam Books, 1975).

6. P.M.H. Atwater, *Beyond the Light: What Isn't Being Said About the Near-Death Experience* (Secaucus, N.J.:Carol Publishing Group, 1994).

7. Ibid.

8. Joseph Head and S. L. Cranston, *Reincarnation: The Phoenix Fire Mystery* (New York: Julian Press, 1994), 450.

9. Henry Wadsworth Longfellow, *The Poems of Longfellow* (Boston: Houghton, Mifflin & Co., 1972).

10. Tom Ball, "The Thinking Universe," *The Mind Body Connection* (Summer 1993), 22.

11. Frederick LeBoyer, *Birth Without Violence* (New York: Knopf, 1975), 26–27.

12. Elisabeth Kubler-Ross, "Interview with Elisabeth Kubler-Ross." *People Magazine* (November 24, 1975).

13. Pierre Teilhard de Chardin, *The Phenomenon of Man* (New York: Harper and Row, 1967), 264–68.

14. Jeffrey Schaub, KPIX-TV, San Francisco, "Near-Death Interview," 1998.

Chapter 7

1. James Lynch, M.D., *The Broken Heart: The Medical Consequences of Loneliness* (New York: Basic Books, 1977).

2. Ibid.

3. Ibid.

4. Dean Ornish, *Love & Survival: 8 Pathways to Intimacy and Health*. New York: Harper Collins, 1999.

5. The results of the Chrysalis Project were presented to Somoma State University as a part of my master's thesis (unpublished).

6. Arthur Janov, *The Feeling Child* (New York: Simon and Schuster, 1973), 199–200.

7. Ibid., 102.

8. Arthur C. Guyton, in his *Textbook of Medical Physiology,* 3rd ed. (Philadelphia: Saunders and Co., 1966, p.1037), describes experiments with mon keys regarding the stimulation of these centers within the hypothalamus. The findings are quite intriguing:

> 1) Prolonged stimulation of the pain center for 24 hours or more causes the animal to become severely sick and actually leads to death.

> 2) Stimulation of the pain center can completely inhibit the pleasure center, illustrating how painful memories can take precedence over and even erase joyful memories.

> 3) Emotional patterns controlling the sympathetic and parasympathetic centers of the hypothalamus can cause wide varieties of peripheral psychosomatic effects.

Chapter 8

1. Frederick Leboyer, *Birth Without Violence* (New York: Knopf, 1975), 78.

2. It was only a few generations ago that many doctors regarded the newborn as a squalling digestive tract, rather than as a loving and deeply feeling human being. The importance of Leboyer's findings is born out by the follow-up work of Dr. Danielle Rapoport, reported in the *New York Times Magazine* by Steven Englund, December 8, 1974.

She studied fifty Leboyer-delivered babies in the early 1960s, ranging in age from eight months to four years old. There is no question in my mind that these children are noticeably different than others who were delivered in the "classical way." They show a markedly greater interest in the world and in people, and they use their intelligence in more positive and socially adaptive ways than other babies do.

3. There appears to be a direct relationship between our feelings of pain, aloneness, and despair, and the emergence of the ego from the rational, action-oriented left brain. It also seems that our connection to love and soul consciousness is mediated through the receptive, feeling/intuitive right brain. Arthur Diekman in *The Nature of Human Consciousness* (edited by Robert Ornstein, San Francisco: W.H. Freeman and Co., 1973, p.68-69) bears this out:

> Consider the experience of love. Here again, the average person has only one word for love, yet he has probably experienced a variety of these love states. We have not developed words for these states because love is experienced in the receptive mode—indeed, it requires the receptive mode for its occurrence. The receptive mode is aimed at maximizing the intake of the environment, and this mode would appear to originate and function maximally in the infant state. The receptive mode is gradually dominated, if not submerged, however, by the progressive development of striving activity in the action mode. In the course of

development, the action mode (left brain) has priority to ensure biological survival.

Also writing in *The Nature of Human Consciousness* (p.97), Michael Gazzaniga comments on the appearance of this left-brain dominance at an early age:

> In the young child, each hemisphere of the brain is about equally developed with respect to language and speech function. We are, thus, faced with the interesting question of why the right hemisphere at an early age and state of development possesses substantial language capacity, whereas at a more adult age, it possesses a rather poor capacity. . . .

The implication is that during maturation, the processes and systems active in making this capacity manifest are somehow inhibited and dismantled in the right hemisphere and allowed to reside only in the left hemisphere. I am convinced that the neurological mechanism responsible for this phenomenon is the pain/reward center in the hypothalamus. Since stimulation of this pain center for 24 hours or more can cause death, and since the ultimate psychic pain is the anguish of being separated from love, then in the face of this anguish encountered in childhood, it stands to reason that the brain must take some action to ensure biological survival.

Thus it follows (since pain and painful memories take precedence over joy and joyful memories) that children begin to deny, mistrust, and forget their original and joyful state of soul consciousness, as the rational (not feeling), action-oriented left brain creates an ego in an effort to repress inner pain and win love and acceptance from outside.

4. In *The Ego and the Id* (translated by Joan Riviere, London: Hogarth Press, 1950, p.31), Sigmund Freud was the first to call the ego a mental projection:

> The ego is ultimately derived from bodily sensations. It may thus be regarded as a mental projection of the surface of the body ... besides representing the superficies (boundary or outer surface) of the mental apparatus.

Freud is really describing the cocoon of ego consciousness, a projection of what we feel we must be in order to be loved and appreciated. The dominant, rational, left brain is in full control and the feeling, intuitive, receptive right brain is submerged beneath fear and pain.

5. Paul Williams, *Das Energi* (New York: Warner, 1973).

6. Carlos Castaneda, *Tales of Power* (New York: Simon and Schuster, 1974), 286.

Chapter 11

1. Pema Chodron, *When Things Fall Apart: Heart Advice for Difficult Times* (Boston: Shambhala, 1997), 34–35.

Chapter 17

1. Milton Avery, *Everyone Has Feelings* (New York: Open Hand Publishing, 1992).

2. This poem is printed on the cover of a music album, *Music of Hope* (New York: Down Under Productions, 2000).

3. Stendhal, *Armance, or Scenes from a Parisian Salon in 1827* (Merlin Press, 1960).

4. Gerald Jampolsky, *Love Is Letting Go of Fear* (Berkeley, CA: Celestial Arts, 1988).

Chapter 18

1. Pierre Teilhard de Chardin, *Le Christique* (Unpublished, 1955).

2. Steven Mitchell, *The Gospel According to Jesus* (New York: Harper Collins, 1991), 10.

3. Ibid.,11.

4. John Ruskin, *Selected Writings* (London: Falcon Press, 1952).

5. Naguib Mahfouz, *The Beginning and the End* (New York: Doubleday, 1990).

Bibliography

Atwater, P.M.H. *Beyond the Light: What Isn't Being Said About the Near-Death Experience.* Secaucus, N.J.: Carol Publishing Group, 1994.

Avery, Milton. *Everyone Has Feelings.* New York: Open Hand Publishing, 1992.

Ball, Tom. "The Thinking Universe." *The Mind Body Connection,* Summer, 1993.

Barnett, Lincoln. *The Universe and Dr. Einstein.* New York: Bantam Books, 1957.

Castaneda, Carlos. *Tales of Power.* New York: Simon and Schuster, 1974.

Chodron, Pema. *When Things Fall Apart: Heart Advice for Difficult Times.* Boston: Shambhala, 1997.

———. *The World As I See It.* Sacramento: Citadel Press, 1993.

Cornell, Eric A., and Carl E. Wieman. "The Bose-Einstein Condensate." *Scientific American,* March 1998.

Eliot, T.S. *Complete Poems and Plays, 1909-1950.* New York: Harcourt Brace, 1976.

Emerson, William, Ph.D. "Infant and Childbirth Refacilitations." Paper presented at a meeting of the Pre- and Perinatal Psychology Assoc. of North America, San Diego, CA, 1985.

Englund, Steven. "Parent and Child." *New York Times Magazine,* December 8, 1974.

Freud, Sigmund. *The Ego and the Id.* Translated by Joan Riviere. London: Hogarth Press, 1950.

Greeley, Andrew M. "The Impossible, It's Happening." *Noetic Sciences Review,* Spring 1988.

Green, Graham. *Reflections.* New York: Viking, 1990.

Greeley, Andrew M., and William McCready. "Are We a Nation of Mystics?" *New York Times Magazine,* January 25, 1975.

Griffin, A., D.W. Snoke, and F.T. Ringari, eds. *Bose-Einstein Condensation.* London: Cambridge University Press, 1995.

Guyton, Arthur C., M.D. *Textbook of Medical Physiology.* 3rd ed. Philadelphia: Saunders and Co., 1966.

Hawking, Steven. *Black Holes and Baby Universes.* New York: Bantam Books, 1993.

Head, Joseph, and S.L. Cranston. *Reincarnation: The Phoenix Fire Mystery.* New York: Julian Press, 1994.

Jampolsky, Gerald. *Love Is Letting Go of Fear.* Berkeley: Celestial Arts, 1988.

Janov, Arthur. *The Feeling Child.* New York: Simon and Schuster, 1973.

Jason, Philip K., ed. *The Anais Nin Reader.* Chicago: Swallow Press, 1973.

Jung, Carl. *Memories, Dreams and Reflections.* New York: Vintage Books, 1963.

Kubler-Ross, Elisabeth. "Interview with Elisabeth Kubler-Ross." *People Magazine,* November 24, 1975.

Leboyer, Frederick. *Birth Without Violence.* New York: Knopf, 1975.

Longfellow, Henry Wadsworth. *The Poems of Longfellow.* New York: Julian Press, 1994.

Lovelock, James. *The Ages of Gaia: A Biography of Our Living Earth.* New York: Norton, 1988.

Lynch, James, M.D. *The Broken Heart: The Medical Consequences of Loneliness.* New York: Basic Books, 1977.

Mahfouz, Naguib. *Beginning and End.* Translated by Ramses Awad, edited by Mason R. Smith. New York: Doubleday, 1989.

Mitchell, Steven. *The Gospel According to Jesus.* New York: Harper Collins, 1991.

Moody, Raymond. *Life After Life.* New York: Bantam Books, 1975.

Nilsson, Lennart. "The First Days of Creation." *Life Magazine,* August 1990.

Ornish, Dean, MD. *Love & Intimacy: 8 Pathways to Intimacy and Health.* New York: Harper Collins, 1998.

Ornstein, Robert. *The Nature of Human Consciousness.* San Francisco: W.H. Freeman and Co., 1973.

Peat, F. David. *Superstrings.* Chicago: Contemporary Books, 1988.

Roland, Allen L. *Conscious Love, the Ultimate Energy.* New York: Vantage Press, 1976.

Ruskin, John. *Selected Writings.* London: Falcon Press, 1952.

Singer, June. *Religion and the Collective Unconscious.* Chicago: Zygon Religious Press, 1969.

Stendhal Robert. *Armance, or Scenes from a Parisian Salon in 1827.* Merlin Press, 1960.

Teilhard de Chardin, Pierre. *Activation of Human Energy.* New York: Harvest, 1970.

——————. *The Future of Man.* New York: Harper, 1964.

——————. *Human Energy.* New York: Harcourt, Brace and Jovanovich, 1962.

——————. *"Le Christique."* Unpublished, 1955.

——————. *The Phenomenon of Man.* New York: Harper and Row, 1967.

Towers, Bernard. *Teilhard de Chardin.* Virginia: John Knox Press, 1966.

Williams, Paul. *Das Energi.* New York: Warner, 1973.

Wordsworth, William. *Complete Poetical Works of Wordsworth.* Boston: Houghton, Mifflin & Co., 1972.

Allen L. Roland, PhD

radical therapy

*Surrender to love
and heal yourself
in seven sessions
(not seven years)*

Give the gift of
radical therapy
to your friends

☐ YES, I want _____ copies of
radical therapy
at $19.95 each — please include
$4.50 shipping for the first book and
$1.00 for each additional book.
CA residents add 7.25% sales tax.

Name _____

Address _____

City _____ State _____ Zip _____

Phone _____

Email _____

Total _____

☐ Check or money order   ☐ Visa   ☐ Mastercard

Card # _____ Exp. _____

Signature _____

Call our Toll Free order line: 1.888.267.4446
Fax your order to: 415.898.1434
Order online: www.OriginPress.com

Please make your check payable and return to:

Origin Press
1122 Grant Avenue, Suite C
Novato, CA 94945

An argument
for self-healing

**Faith and
the Placebo
Effect**

Lolette Kuby

"A brilliant and important guide to encourage us to accept full responsibility for our thoughts."
—Barbara Marx Hubbard, author of Conscious Evolution

Lolette Kuby
Faith and the Placebo Effect
An argument for self-healing

☐ YES, I want _____ copies of
Faith and the Placebo Effect
at $23 USA and $35 Canada—
please include:
$4.50 shipping for the first book and
$1.00 for each additional book.
CA residents add 7.25% sales tax.

Name _____

Address _____

City _____ State ____ Zip _____

Phone _____

Email _____

Total _____

☐ Check or money order   ☐ Visa   ☐ Mastercard

Card # _____ Exp. _____

Signature _____

Call our Toll Free order line: 1.888.267.4446
Fax your order to: 415.898.1434
Order online: www.OriginPress.com

Please make your check payable and return to:

Origin Press
1122 Grant Avenue, Suite C
Novato, CA 94945